The Gurkha War

The Gurkha War

The Anglo-Nepalese Conflict in
North East India 1814-1816

H. T. Prinsep

LEONAUR

The Gurkha War: the Anglo-Nepalese Conflict
in North East India 1814-1816
by H. T. Prinsep

First published in 1825 in
History of the Political and Military Transactions in India
During the Administration of the Marquess of Hastings
1813 - 1823, vol 1

FIRST EDITION

Published by Leonaur Ltd

ISBN: 978-1-84677-169-9 (hardcover)
ISBN: 978-1-84677-170-5 (softcover)

http://www.leonaur.com

Publisher's Notes

Contents

Publisher's Note

For more than 150 years the soldiers from Nepal—the Ghurkhas—have been an essential part of the British Army. They are unique. Their courage, humour, generosity and loyalty have no parallels in British military history. They have been at the forefront of conflict in the cause of Crown and Empire during many of the wars for the Indian sub-continent and beyond. Through the Great War, the Second World War, the small wars of the post WWII period and, in more recent times, as part of peace-keeping missions, they have rendered invaluable service to the British.

Of all the British colonial warriors, only the Ghurkhas have retained their place fighting alongside their regular army comrades and, such is their fame and the esteem in which they are held, they still hold a place in the hearts of every soldier who serves with them, and, incredibly, with the British public as well.

It was not always so! In the early nineteenth century and before, the Kingdom of Nepal was a power to be reckoned with on the sub-continent. As the British expanded their empire many martial races came into conflict with them and their native armies. The Moguls, Mahrattas, Rajputs and Pindarees were amongst the formidable opponents the British encountered; and in the north west of the sub-continent the Sikhs of the Punjab ruled over massive lands beyond the Sutlej. At the time of the events recounted in this book, their inevitable collision with the British had not yet occurred, but the Nepalese—occupying territories far beyond their present day mountainous state—were making their presence felt by resisting the relentless occupation of the British in the north east.

At this time the Nepalese were no less formidable as fighters than they have been in subsequent decades fighting alongside the British. There was one fundamental difference however, for at that time the Ghurkhas and the British were implacable enemies.

This is the story of the Ghurkha War, a conflict between peoples who would come to be bound by unbreakable bonds of friendship and respect—an alliance forged in animosity. Very little has been has been written about this unique and unusual war and this Leonaur book is both essential reading for those with an interest in the history of the period and a true first.

The Leonaur Editors

INTRODUCTION
Causes of the Nepal War

The state of Nepal and the circumstances which brought
it into contact with the British government have no direct
connexion with the states and powers of central India; its
conduct as a nation had made war inevitable, even before
Lord Hastings had set foot in the country.

It is foreign to our design to attempt any consistent relation of the means and gradations by which the Goorkhas
had risen to power in the mountainous tract stretching between the plains of Hindoostan and the high lands of Tar-
tary and Tibet. Suffice it to say, that when Lord Hastings
took charge of the supreme government, he found their
dominion to extend as far as the river Teesta to the east, and
westward to the Sutlej; so that this nation was then in actual
possession of the whole of the strong country which skirts
the northern frontier of Hindoostan.

This extent of dominion had been acquired entirely
during the last fifty years, by the systematic prosecution
of a policy likened by the Goorkhas themselves, and not
inaptly so, to that which had gained for us the empire of
Hindoostan. The hill Rajas, whom they had successively
conquered and displaced, were mere ignorant, selfish ty-
rants, on bad terms with their subjects and neighbours, but
most of all, with their own relations. Thus, while there was
amongst them no principle of combination for mutual de-

fence against a common enemy, not one of the petty prin-
cipalities was sufficiently strong or united within itself to be
capable of substantial resistance.

The Goorkha chiefs were at all times as ready to apply the
influence of intrigue as open force, and could well combine
both for the prosecution of their ends. They had a regular
army, obedient to its officers, and the whole in proper subor-
dination to the state. This was always available to the weaker
party upon conditions, and the frequent internal dissensions
of the Rajas, which successively came to form the Goorkha
frontier, never failed to produce the invitation.

Prithee Nurayun Sah has the merit of establishing the
system which raised this nation to power. Taught by the
example of our early victories in Bengal, he armed and dis-
ciplined a body of troops after the English fashion; and after
a struggle of more than ten years, finally subjugated the valley of Nepal by their means in 1768. The Moorshedabad
Nuwab (Kasim Ulee Khan) attempted to interfere in 1762-
3, but sustained a signal defeat under the walls of Mukwanpoor; and the British government was not more successful
in an effort made some years after to succour the last of the
Sooruj Bunsee dynasty, who reigned at Katmandoo.*

Prithee Nurayun dying in 1771, his son Singh Purtap,

---

* The expedition was undertaken at the recommendation of Mr. Golding,
the commercial agent at Betia, who feared that the success of the Goorkhas
would ruin the trade he before carried on with Nepal: it had been interrupt-
ed for three or four years in consequence of the subjugation of Mukwanpoor.
Major Kinloch commanded the party destined for the relief of the Nepal
Raja. He was a good officer: but advanced into the hills a month at least too
early (in October 1767), and had not strength enough to establish a chain
of depots to secure his communication with the plains; consequently, having
penetrated to Hureehurpoor, he was detained there by a *nulla*, not fordable,
and the bridge and raft he constructed were carried away after a fall of rain,
which swelled the torrent unnaturally. The delay thus experienced exhausted
his supplies, and produced sickness; so that, finally, he was obliged to return
early in December—the time when, properly, he should have set out.

and, in 1775, his grandson Run Buhadur came successively to the throne; the latter, however, being an infant, Buhadur Sah, another son of Prithee Nurayun, struggled long with his brother's widow for the regency. Her death at last gave him the ascendancy, which he kept till 1795; when Run Buhadur came of age, and forcibly assumed the sceptre to the destruction of his uncle.

Run Buhadur, proving a tyrant, was expelled in 1800, and took refuge for a time at Bunarus. In the interval of his exile, the Bengal government established a commercial treaty with the ruling faction; and Captain Knox was sent resident to Katmandoo in 1802. Colonel Kirkpatrick had before been employed on a mission to that capital by Lord Cornwallis, but was obliged to return without effecting any thing; and the same jealousy of the object with which the connexion was sought by us being still alive, Captain Knox was recalled, and the connexion broken off in 1804.

Run Buhadur left Bunarus, and was receive again with open arms by his subjects of Katmandoo, soon after Captain Knox's recall; but his disposition proved to be incorrigibly tyrannical; his bad propensities had been exasperated rather than chastened by adversity, and by the restraints of a residence within the British frontier. The principal people of the court therefore, who found themselves the objects of a revengeful persecution, a second time formed a conspiracy against the Raja, which was brought to a desperate issue prematurely. The conspirators, having some reason to apprehend that they were betrayed, suddenly resolved to sell their lives as dearly as possible; and one of them, the Raja's half brother, rushed forward and cut Run Buhadur down nearly to the middle by a blow of his *koka*,* as he sat in full *durbar* in 1805. A barbarous affray followed, in which the

---

* The *koka* is a short but heavy sword, the edge of which is on the inner side, like that of a scythe.

brother was himself slain with most of the chief men of the state, and the royal family was nearly extinguished. An infant son of Run Buhadur's was, however, with difficulty secreted in the women's apartments, and thus saved from the massacre by Bheem Sein Thapa, who proclaimed him a few days after, by the name of Kurman Jodh Bikrum Sah, and who, by his influence with the regent-mother, succeeded in introducing himself to a large share in the government.

The Raja was still in his minority when the war broke out with the British; and the power of the state was in the hands of an aristocracy, composed of the highest military officers, with whom were associated some of the Raja's distant relations, and some Brahmins. The Panres, or Pandees, were at the head of the faction which had expelled Run Buhadur, in 1800, but on that chief's return, they were for the most part cut off or expatriated; and since then the Thapas had acquired the paramount authority, Bheem Sein Thapa, who assumed and still uses the English title of General, had the principal conduct of affairs at the capital. He was the son of a chief named Kajee Umur Singh Thapa, governor of Palpa on the Gourukhpoor frontier, and who died in October 1814.

All the territory held by the Goorkhas west of the Gogra had been acquired within the last fifteen years, by the arms of another Umur Singh Thapa; who, having been for many years at the head of a successful army, had clothed himself with a power, which the nationality of his troops and his own patriotism alone prevented him from making independent. The terms on which he stood towards those who conducted affairs at Katmandoo, and the politics of the court, generally, will be better understood from what we shall presently have to relate: we shall first state briefly the nature and origin of the disputes which ultimately brought on the war.

The whole range of hills is skirted along it southern base by a magnificent forest, chiefly Sal trees, (*Shorea Robusta*). The timber is useful in ship-building, though far inferior to the teak of Malabar, and of the Burman empire. The boats, however, which navigate the upper Ganges, and the beams and rafters for building throughout Hindoostan, even down to Calcutta, are almost exclusively made of it. The forest therefore is valuable*; it abounds in elephants, which are chiefly prized for their teeth, the animals being less fit for carriage, and in other respects greatly inferior to what are caught at Chittagong, Ceylon, and in the countries nearer the Line. Beyond the forest, towards Hindoostan, is an open plain, called the Turaee or Tereeana, which is chiefly valuable on account of the fine pasture it yields during the months of April and May, when the periodical hot winds entirely destroy the herbage of the more southern regions. The bunjaree bullocks from Malwa, and even from the northern parts of the Dukhun, come here to graze in those months; and the *Kahchuraee*, or pasturage-rate, levied by the border Zemindars, is a very productive branch of their revenue.

The soil of the Turaee is for the most part extremely rich; and though the number of wild elephants, rhinoceroses, and buffaloes that find shelter in the adjoining forest, makes it very uncertain whether the husbandman will reap the fruits of his tillage, cultivation has nevertheless made rapid advances there. The insalubrity of the climate during a great portion of the year, prevents the establishment of any considerable towns in the tract. The population is, indeed, for the most part migratory; the several classes retiring either into the hills, or to a distance in the plains, when the unhealthy season commences. There are

---

*It is a saying of the Goorkhas, that every tree is a mine of gold.

ruins, however, at Sumroun, and in other parts of the Turaee, which would seem to indicate that, at some former period, the capital of an extensive province was situated there, and that the tract therefore was not always so unhealthy as it is now deemed; but nothing satisfactory on this head has yet been ascertained.

From time immemorial, the country within the hills and on the borders has been divided amongst petty Hindoo Rajas, and the forest and Turaee have naturally been a perpetual bone of contention to them; a chieftain possessing fastnesses in the hills could always enforce contributions, by issuing thence and carrying off booty from those who hesitated to comply. Hence every hill Raja had a sweep of the forest and low country attached to his estate, and this he was continually endeavouring to extend, either by intrigue, or by violence, or by any means that presented. The superior wealth and greater number of followers at the command of some of the Rajas of the plains, enabled them occasionally to penetrate and reduce to subjection a hill neighbour; but ordinarily, such enterprizes were beyond their skill or resources; and the border-war was handed down from father to son, in their respective families.

Neither Ukbur nor any of his descendants on the throne of Dehlee made any attempt to add the tract of hills to the Moghul empire; its revenue was not an object of cupidity, nor was its population sufficiently formidable to make the subjugation of the country necessary as an act of political precaution. The Rajas of the plains, on the other hand, though compelled to submit to the Moosulman yoke, retained their territories, and became tributaries of the empire; which did not prevent their prosecuting their hereditary feuds with their neighbours in the hills, in the same manner as heretofore. The Moghul officers, not sorry to see a powerful vassal weakened, would sometimes foment these disputes, and make grants of their tributary's lands in the plains, for the aggrandizement of a hill Raja; whose name would thus be added to the list of subjects. Ordinarily, however, the Soobas did not interfere in the management of the affairs of this remote tract. The Rajas, therefore, were at perfect liberty to pursue their old system; and such continued to be the state of this frontier, until the low countries fell under the British dominion, and the hills were gradually overrun by the Nepalese, and consolidated by them into one sovereignty.

The British government, assimilating its conduct to that of its predecessors, did not interfere with the possessions of the Rajas in the plains; but contented itself with a money-tribute, or at least with a composition for the rights asserted by the Moghuls, which becoming fixed in amount at the perpetual settlement, may be so described.

The Goorkhas, on the other hand, as each Raja in the hills successively fell before them, exterminated the family; and, becoming heir to all its possessions, took up likewise the old Raja's claims and contests with his neighbours. This brought them into contact with our Zemindars, who were, of course, unable to maintain themselves against such an enemy, and generally therefore had to resign the object in dispute; for, unless when the encroachment was gross and easy of proof, it was vain to hope to interest British government in their favour. That government was, in the first place, no loser by the usurpation, for the public revenue was fully secured by the perpetual settlement, and by the increased value of the entire estate against any loss from a partial aggression. Moreover, it was on principle, distrustful of the pretensions of its own subjects, which were generally exaggerated; while it regarded the Goorkha nation as a well disposed neighbour, whom it was desirable to conciliate; hence an injured Raja of the plains would seldom succeed in procuring any powerful support to his cause, unless, as above observed, the case were very flagrant, when the Goorkhas would on remonstrance make reparation.

It will be proper to illustrate this view by an appeal to facts; and the disputes on the Sarun frontier, one of the main causes of the war, afford a case strongly in point.

The Raja of Chumparun, who resides at Betia, was perpetually at war with the Raja of Mukwanpoor within the hills, for different portions of the Turaee; and amongst other sources of dispute, each of them had pretensions to sovereignty over part of a Perguna called Sumroun, the same in which the ruins before alluded to are situated. We shall endeavour to explain the circumstances of this dispute with some minuteness, at the risk of appearing tedious.

The Mukwanpoor family granted Roteehut and Puchroutee, two *tuppas* (subdivisions) of the above Perguna, in Jageer to Ubdoollah Beg, a Moosulman, who had influence enough with the Moorshedabad family to get there a confirmation of the tenure by the Nazim. The Betia Raja, who had claims on the tract, and was, there is reason to believe, then in possession, at first resisted; but in the end, gave likewise to Ubdoollah a *sunud** for the same lands. Thus was the Moosulman's tenure secured, to whichever party the right belonged; but as the Mukwanpoor grant was the oldest in date, and had been acknowledged at Moorshedabad, this Raja's title to resume eventually acquired a kind of preference. In 1763, Prithee Nurayun, having subdued the Mukwanpoor Raja, claimed to be feudal superior over Ubdoollah; and resolved, as soon as he had secured his conquest, to resume the Jageer. Accordingly, after a year or two, he seized not only Ubdoollah's lands, but twenty-two villages more, which

---

* *Sunud*, a deed of gift

he claimed to be part of Roteehut, though not in the Jageerdar's possession.

Ubdoollah fled to the English authorities; who took up his cause, and made his injuries one pretext for the declaration of war issued prior to the advance of Major Kinloch in 1767. This officer, having failed in penetrating into the hills, was desired to occupy the whole Turaee, as a means of remunerating the British government for the expense incurred. Ubdoollah then claimed his Jageer, and Roteehut and Puchroutee were in consequence given up to him. When peace was restored with the Nepalese, they sent an agent named Deenanath to claim the territory given up to Ubdoollah Beg as part of Mukwanpoor. This was opposed by the Betia Raja, and a long investigation ensued; when, upon the strength of the first deed of grant to Ubdoollah, which was on copper, and of a date falling in 1743, Mr. Hastings finally decided, in 1781, that Roteehut and Puchroutee belonged to Mukwanpoor, and were not parcel of Betia or Chumparun.

While this contest was undetermined, the Goorkhas courted Ubdoollah, and promised to maintain him, for without his help their title could not have been established. After it was decided, however, they resumed his Jageer, and occupied it for themselves. The twenty-two villages seized, on the first invasion of the Goorkhas, on pretence of their belonging to Roteehut, had never been given up either to Ubdoollah, or to the Nepalese; and no demand was ever made for them. On the contrary, from the time of Major Kinloch's occupation, in January 1768, the revenue of them was uniformly collected as parcel of the Tuppa of Nunnor, or Noor; belonging equally with Roteehut to the Perguna of Sumroun, but falling in that portion of it which was annexed to Chumparun.

At the perpetual settlement concluded by the British

government in 1790, Nunnor formed part of the lands for which the Raja of Betia engaged: and thus the matter stood on this frontier till 1810: the twenty-two villages continuing all the while in this Raja's possession.

From the above statement it will be seen that Roteehut, which appears to have originally belonged to the Raja of the plains, was finally dismembered from his territory, and annexed to the hills, by the effect of the intrigue of the hill Raja with Ubdoollah Beg. It was even more common, however, for a hill Raja to become possessed of. an estate by usurpation, and then to have his title acknowledged by being permitted to engage for the revenue. The offer of an advance in the yearly rate, or a present payment in cash, was always sufficient to effect such an arrangement with a temporary Amil: and after once procuring possession, with an acknowledged title, all future payments were of course dependent on circumstances, and the interest of the moment.

Of the confusion incident to this conduct in native Amils, more than one instance was brought to light upon our occupying the territory ceded by the Nuwab Vizeer in 1801. The most notable was that of the Raja of the independent hill territory of Palpa, who had contrived to possess himself of Bootwul, lying for the most part in the plains; for the revenue of which he accounted to the Nuwab Vizeer's government. In like manner the Goorkhas themselves had usurped Sheeoraj on the same frontier; and they further held two Talooks, called Tilpoor and Bunaeekpoor, by the same sufferance; professing to be accountable for the revenue, though they paid or not, according to circumstances.

The Bootwul case requires particular mention. On our first occupying Gourukpoor, the Raja of Palpa's family had been recently driven out of the further hills, and obliged to take refuge in Bootwul, which is situated in the mouth of the first pass. At the settlement of the district in 1801-2, the Raja's manager engaged to us, as he had heretofore done to the Oudh government, for the lands of Bootwul, at a *juma*, or annual assessment, of 32,000 rupees. The Raja himself was then at Katmandoo, negotiating about his territory in the hills. He came, however, to the plains shortly after, and confirmed the engagement with the British Collector, which had been entered into by his manager.

The Goorkhas subsequently induced him to return to Katmandoo, where he was committed to prison, and in the end put to death. The family upon this, fearing the continued enmity of the Goorkhas if they resided on the frontier, obtained permission to give up Bootwul to the Company's *Khas*, or special management, and took up their residence at the station of Gourukpoor, upon a pension being assigned to them in *lieu* of their profit from the management of the estate.

The Goorkhas in 1804, on the ground of having subdued the Palpa Raja, claimed Bootwul as part of his territory. They immediately, therefore, begun sending people to collect the rents, instead of allowing them to be received by the company's manager. By November 1805, they had established their influence over two-thirds of the Perguna; but the circumstance having been brought to Sir G. Barlow's notice, when he was at Allahabad in that year, he addressed a letter to the court at Katmandoo, calling upon them to evacuate Bootwul; and giving them to understand that the company's right to the sovereignty of Sheeoraj also was undoubted—the Talook being included by name amongst the Oudh cessions, and the Goorkhas having no title but that of usurpation. Since, however, the date of the seizure of this place was anterior to our possession of Gourukpoor, Sir George professed a willingness to give up his claim to Sheeoraj, on the condition of the instant evacuation of

Bootwul. The Goorkhas answered this by an offer to farm Bootwul as a Zemindaree, on the terms agreed to by the Raja and his manager at the first settlement: this, however, was refused, and instant evacuation ordered. But Sir G. Barlow, having shortly afterwards gone as governor to Madras, and Lord Minto's attention being occupied with other things, the matter remained for some years without further notice; and, in the mean time, the Goorkhas occupied the whole of Bootwul.

Emboldened by the indifference thus manifested, in 1810-1, they crossed the small river that forms the boundary of Bootwul, and began to occupy some villages of the adjoining Perguna of Palee. They also advanced from Sheeoraj, till at last their encroachments in this quarter again attracted the attention of government; and in the beginning of 1812, after remonstrating against the aggressions, Lord Minto repeated Sir G. Barlow's offer, to resign his right to Sheeoraj, on condition of the immediate evacuation of Bootwul and all subsequent occupations. Bheem Sein's father, Umur Singh, who was now the Goorkha governor of Palpa, answered the proposition on this occasion by asserting a distinct right to all he had taken, and even to more.

This circumstance, combined with what occurred simultaneously on the Sarun frontier, induced the British government to nominate a Commissioner, and to invite the Goorkhas to send others to meet him, in order to settle finally the boundary line of the respective territories. Considering that the peremptory demand made by Sir G. Barlow in 1805 for the evacuation of Bootwul, had been answered by an offer to farm it, which was a distinct admission of our right, the nomination of a Commission to investigate the matter now, before enforcing the evacuation, was an act of most exemplary and undeserved moderation.

What had passed, however, on the Sarun frontier remains to be told. The lands forming the Jageer of Ubdoollah remained, as resigned by Mr. Hastings, in the hands of the Nepalese, without aggression on the Betia territory, till the end of 1810, as has been before-mentioned. In 1811, one Luchungeer, the Goorkha Sooba (governor) of Roteehut, crossed the frontier with a party of armed men; and having seized and stockaded Kewya, one of the twenty-two* villages occupied in Prithee Nurayun's time, began plundering and making collections in eight others of them, stating that they belonged to Roteehut. The Raja of Betia's people resisted this aggression, and an affray followed, in which Luchungeer was killed. This occurred on the 19th of June, 1811.

The British government, on first hearing of the circumstance, directed the assistant to the Magistrate of Sarun to proceed to the frontier, in order to inquire into the particulars of the affray; but, before he arrived there, a reinforcement had been sent down from Katmandoo, which immediately seized on the whole of the twenty-two villages. Mr. Young's proceedings were, therefore, confined to the ascertainment of this fact, and of the circumstances of Luchungeer's death; both which being established, he submitted his report, and returned to Sarun. In this stage, the case was referred for the investigation of the Commissioner, whom it had already been resolved to send to Gourukpoor, and the instructions as to the further measures to be adopted were addressed to him.

---

* As these twenty-two villages are continually recurring, it may be useful to give their names, and to state that they all lie to the South of the ruins of Sumroun:—1. Bijbunee; 2. Atmoha; 3. Gora Suhun; 4. Sree Nugur, a Tola; 5. Kewya, or Byrajputee; 6. Poornyhia; 7. Korya; 8. Sumunpoor; 9. Busuntpoor; 10. Bejaee; 11. Bhulooa; 12. Kudumooa; 13. Bunkutwa; 14. Nemya; 15. Pukureea; 16. Kurwa; 17. Ambooa, a Tola; 18. Jujhoora; 19. Gogawa; 20. Simree; 21. Khujuaree; 22. Chynpoor, a Tola of Kurwa, No. 16.

Major Paris Bradshaw, first Assistant to the Resident at Lukhnou, was the person nominated by Lord Minto to settle these frontier disputes; and in the season 1812-13 he met the Goorkha Commissioners in the Gourukpoor part of the Turaee, and proceeded first to investigate the title they preferred to Bootwul and Sheeoraj.

The inquiry was extended to both estates, in consequence of the court at Katmandoo not having closed with either of our offers to resign the latter conditionally.

The result of the investigation established the facts above related, in regard to Bootwul, beyond the possibility of doubt. Sheeoraj was proved to have been seized by the Goorkhas sixteen years before the cession of Gourukpoor to us; and great importance was attached by them to some *perwanas*, or written orders, addressed by British commanders to the Goorkha Sooba, at the time of Vizeer Ulee's flight from Bunarus to the Turaee, after the murder of Mr. Cherry, in 1798. They argued that the demand then made of aid for that delinquent's apprehension, implied an acknowledgment of right to the territory within which the exertion was called for. The documents were certainly evidence to the power and possession of the Goorkhas; two points which were not denied; but for ten of the sixteen years they had held Sheeoraj, the revenue had been accounted for to the Amils of the Nuwab Vizeer's government, while the origin of the Goorkha title was clearly traced to open usurpation.

The investigation having been brought to this issue, Major Bradshaw was instructed to demand the evacuation both of Bootwul and Sheeoraj. The Goorkha Commissioners declared themselves not satisfied, and begged to refer the; matter to Katmandoo. The Major accordingly submitted his proceedings for the orders of his government, while he himself went on to the Sarun frontier.

Here it was in his instructions that he should insist on the restitution of the twenty-two villages occupied in 1811, as a preliminary to any investigation of the claim set up by the Goorkhas. After much evasion, he procured this; but when he proposed opening the inquiry, the Nepalese Commissioners, affecting to have taken some personal offence against the Major, refused to have more discussion with him, and suddenly returned to Katmandoo, leaving him alone on the frontier.

This occurred in March 1814, and was evidently a result of the determination formed by the Goorkha government upon the Gourukpoor cases, which had previously been brought to issue.

Lord Minto, being perfectly satisfied with the proceedings forwarded by Major Bradshaw, addressed a letter to the Raja, in June, 1813, demanding the immediate evacuation both of Bootwul and Sheeoraj. The answer to this did not arrive till December: it was replete with fulsome professions of respect and attachment; but declared the right of the Goorkhas to both Bootwul and Sheeoraj to have been clearly established by the result of the investigation. No reasons were assigned, and as far as concerned Bootwul at least, the assertion seemed to be in the face of all the evidence.

Lord Hastings, who had in the interval assumed charge of the government, as soon as he had examined the voluminous proceedings and papers, and made himself master of the case, Addressed to the Raja of Nepal a peremptory requisition to evacuate the two districts; and he sent the letter through the Magistrate of Gourukpoor, giving that officer authority to order the advance of a body of troops to occupy the contested lands, in case the Raja's order for their evacuation should not arrive within twenty-five days from the date of his forwarding the letter. The Goorkha government was further informed that the Magistrate had these orders.

It was the receipt of this letter that had produced the sensation at Katmandoo, which occasioned the sudden recall of the Commissioners from Sarun, and ended in the resolution to abide the issue of war. In April 1814, a council was held, at which the Goorkha Commissioners from the frontier, and two and twenty others of the principal people of the court, were present, and the question of war or peace was fairly debated, in a sitting which lasted from nine o'clock in the morning till eight at night.

There were some in the council who had apprehensions of the result; but an overweening confidence in their own power and resources, and the opinion of their entire invulnerability in the hills prevailed.* The advocates of war, indeed, argued that by remaining in their native fastnesses, and issuing thence on predatory excursions into the plains, a state of war could be made even more profitable and advantageous, than peace would be with the loss of the power of encroaching with impunity.

The Goorkhas, as before stated, came to this resolution in April; they gave, however, no intimation of their hostile intentions, and answered the Governor-General's letter on the subject of Bootwul and Sheeoraj, by mere commonplace assurances of respect, and of a desire to keep on a good understanding with the British, omitting all mention of the specific subject in discussion.

In the mean time, Sir Roger Martin, the Gourukpoor Magistrate, receiving no orders from Katmandoo for the evacuation of the disputed districts, addressed the commanding officer at the station; and on the expiration of the period, three companies marched to occupy the lands. The Goorkha officers retired before them, without making the slightest opposition. For nearly a month, too, that

* In the Appendix a curious report of the opinions of some of the chiefs, as forwarded to the Palpa governor, with instructions to prepare for war.

the troops remained in the Turaee, they attempted nothing; but suffered the magistrate to establish three police *thanas* in Bootwul, at Chitwa, Bisourea, and Sourah, and one with two subordinate outposts at Sheeoraj, without even making a remonstrance against the manner of occupation. The above arrangement was made merely with a view to the ordinary administration of the districts, upon the retirement of the troops, and wholly without anticipation of attack or hostility of any kind on the part of the Goorkhas.

Early on the morning of the 29th May, 1814, before the regular troops had reached Gourukpoor on their return, the three *thanas* of Bootwul were surrounded simultaneously, and the people attacked without warning. At the three stations eighteen men were killed and four wounded; the *daroga*, or chief officer of the *thana* of Chitwa, was murdered in cold blood, after he had surrendered, and in the presence of Munraj, the late Goorkha governor of Bootwul, who was the leader of this enterprise. As the season was too far advanced for our troops to take the field, the magistrate ordered his *thanas* in Sheeoraj to concentrate and retire on Bansee; thus relinquishing for the present all he had occupied. One of the outposts was, however, surprised at Rourah on the 3rd of June, when four men more were killed and two wounded by the Nepalese.

While hostilities were thus commencing in Gourukpoor, the disputes on the Sarun frontier were fast coming to the same issue. The Marquess of Hastings, on first hearing of the conduct of the Nepalese Commissioners, ordered the permanent annexation to the British territories of the twenty-two villages, and the other disputed tracts of that frontier; and he sent a force of a few companies, which remained in the Turaee during the rains, to secure this quarter. The formal declaration of war was purposely delayed till the close of the rains, in order to allow time for persons engaged in trade with Nepal to withdraw their capital, as well as to give the Nepalese the opportunity of disavowing the act of Munraj, and punishing the perpetrators, if so inclined. They showed no disposition to do so; but, on the contrary, made the most active military preparations along the whole extent of their frontier. The declaration of war was accordingly at length issued by his Lordship from Lukhnou, on the 1st November, 1814.

The aggressions on the Sarun and Gourukpoor frontiers are the only ones that have been related at length, and were doubtless the most important; but there were innumerable others equally unwarranted, along the whole Turaee. The magistrate of Tirhoot reported, that between 1787 and 1813 upwards of two hundred villages had been seized on one or other unjustifiable pretext. On the Purneah frontier, the Goorkha governor of Morung had, in 1808, seized the whole Zemindaree of Bheemnugur; but this case being particularly flagrant, was taken up immediately, and in June 1809, a detachment under an officer was sent to the frontier, when the Nepalese, yielding to the threat of an immediate appeal to the sword, evacuated the lands in the course of 1810.

Towards Rohilkhund the Goorkhas had seized five of eight Talooks, composing the Perguna of Khyreegurh: three of which were taken before and two after the cession to us in 1801. They also advanced a claim to Kasheepoor, and other lands of Moradabad; but were deterred from seizing them. In the Seikh country, beyond the Jumna, Umur Singh, the Goorkha commander, was engaged in hostilities with Sunsar-Chund, of Kankra, and with other hill Rajas, who held likewise lands in the plains; to which, as each successively fell before him, he advanced a claim. In 1813 he came down and seized some villages on this plea; but on receiving a vigorous remonstrance from Major-General, then Colonel, Ochterlony, who commanded at Loodheeana, he retired. It appeared, indeed, that both his situation and general views of policy made him averse to pushing things to extremity with the British; and he early expressed a decided opinion against the measures adopted in Bootwul and Sheeoraj, which he declared to have originated in the selfish views of persons, who scrupled not to involve the nation in war to gratify their personal avarice.* The insinuation was levelled at Bheem Sein, whose father had made the usurpation, and whose family derived most of the advantages.

The revenue of the usurped lands, it is to be observed, could not have been less than a *lack* of rupees a year to the Goorkhas, taken altogether, in the manner they collected it: the retention of this income was therefore an object of no small importance to the ambitious views of Bheem Sein, and to the preservation of the influence he had contrived to establish for his family.

---

*Vide Umur Singh's opinion in reply to the question submitted by the Raja, Appendix A.; also his intercepted letter, B.

CHAPTER 1

The Formidable Foe

The Marquess of Hastings, very soon after his arrival in India, determined to make a tour of inspection to the western provinces. Accordingly, in prosecution of this intention, he embarked at Calcutta in June 1814, and reached Cawnpoor (Kanhpoor) by the end of September, after a tedious navigation up the Ganges.

The discussion with the Nepalese had been brought to issue by the murder of the police-officers in Gourukpoor, a short time before his Lordship left the presidency. The interval of the journey, therefore, was employed in preparation for the vigorous prosecution of the war in the hills, and in defensive arrangements against the probability of another violation of our frontier by the Pindarees. The leaders of those associations might, it was thought, be tempted to seize the opportunity to annoy us that would be afforded by the employment of our troops in the opposite direction. The nature, however, of the defensive arrangements resolved upon will be explained hereafter. First, we shall relate the occurrences of the campaign in the hills, and it will be convenient to pursue them without interruption from their commencement in October 1814, to the close of the campaign in April of the following year.

The frontier which was to be the scene of war stretched a distance of about six hundred miles; and the enemy had the command of all the passes of the forest, as well as the hills. This, and the general suspiciousness of the Goorkha character, rendered it extremely difficult for Lord Hastings to collect intelligence for the arrangement of his plan of operations. He, nevertheless, resolved to act offensively against the enemy along the whole line of frontier, from the Sutlej to the Koosee; and the following was the allotment ultimately made of this space to the several divisions that were brought into the field. It was assigned to Colonel Ochterlony,* who commanded the post established at Loodheeana in 1808-9, to operate in the hilly country lying near the Sutlej. The force under this officer's command was exclusively Native Infantry and artillery, and amounted to about six thousand men; it had a train of two 18-pounders, ten 6-pounders, and four mortars and howitzers.

From Meeruth in the Dooab, Major-General Gillespie, whose conduct at Vellore and in Java had given his name a high celebrity, was to proceed first against the Dehra Doon (a rich valley stretching between the Ganges and Jumna, within the firsts range of hills), and as soon as this should be reduced, which it was expected would not be an operation of much time or difficulty, the force was to divide; and while a detachment attacked Gurhwal and Sirinugur, under the snowy range, the main body was to proceed against Nahn, to the west of the Jumna, in aid of the operations of Major-General Ochterlony against Umur Singh. General Gillespie's force originally consisted of His Majesty's 53rd, which, with artillery and a few dismounted Dragoons, made up about one thousand Europeans, and two thousand five hundred Native Infantry.

This division, and that under General Ochterlony, were

---

* This officer's commission of Major-General arrived soon after the opening of the campaign; we shall therefore henceforth designate him as of that rank.

ordered to take the field towards the end of October; the unhealthy season of the rains being generally over to the north-west by the beginning or middle of this month. Kumaon, and Almora, its capital, were to be attacked from Rohilkhund; but, according to the original plan, this movement was to follow the occupation of Gurhwal to the north of the province; and the operations undertaken here in December and January were an afterthought, suggested by the peculiar circumstances that attended the commencement of the war.

From Bunarus and Gourukpoor a force was collected, and placed under the command of Major-General John Sullivan Wood, and his instructions were to penetrate by Bootwul into Palpa. This division consisted of His Majesty's 17th foot, nine hundred and fifty strong, and about three thousand Native Infantry; it had a train of seven 6 and 3-pounders, and four mortars and howitzers. The 15th of November was fixed upon as the day on which this force was to take the field at Gourukpoor.

Further east from Patna and Moorshedabad, another force of a strength of near eight thousand men, including His Majesty's 24th foot, nine hundred and seven strong, was collected for the main attack, which was intended to be made direct upon the capital of Katmandoo by the passes between the Gunduk and Bagmuttee. Major-General Marley was intrusted with the command of this army, and there was a train attached to it of four 18-pounders, eight 6 and 3-pounders, and fourteen mortars and howitzers. The Ganges was to be crossed by the troops from Patna on the 15th of November; and a further brigade was formed, from troops at more distant stations, to follow the army and secure its depots and rear, as it advanced into the hills.

Beyond the Koosee eastward, Major Latter was furnished with two thousand men, including his district battalion, for the defence of the Poornea frontier. This officer was desired to open a communication with the petty Raja of Sikhim, and to give him every assistance and encouragement to expel the Goorkhas from the eastern hills, short of an actual advance of troops for the purpose. The Raja's minister had invited the common enemy, who thus had acquired a footing at Nagree and in the pass of Nagurkot; but little advance had yet been made by the Nepalese in the subjugation of the country, and the struggle with the Raja's adherents was still actively going on when the declaration of war issued. Sikhim is tributary to Lassa and the Chinese: the frontier towards the plains is small, being bounded by the Teesta to the east, and by the Michee to the west; but the territory extends northward to the snowy range, and was found to afford a more ready communication with Lassa and China than that through Bootan, by which route Messrs. Bogle and Turner penetrated in Mr. Hastings' time.

Such were the dispositions made for the campaign. Major-General Gillespie was the first to penetrate the enemy's frontier. On the 22nd of October he seized the Keree pass leading into the Doon, and thence proceeded to Dehra, the principal town in the valley, without meeting any opposition. The whole of the hill country, west of the Ganges, was still under Umur Singh; who had allotted a force of about six hundred men under the command of Captain*

---

* The use of English terms for their grades of command was general in the Goorkha army, but the powers of the different ranks did not correspond with those of our system. The title of General was assumed by Bheem Sein, as Commander-in-chief, and enjoyed by himself alone; of Colonels, there were three or four only; all principal officers of the court, commanding more than one battalion. The title of Major was held by the adjutant of a battalion or independent company; and Captain was the next grade to colonel, implying the command of a corps. *Luftun*, or Lieutenant, was the style of the officers commanding companies under the Captain; and then followed the subaltern ranks of *Soobadar, Jemadar*, and *Havildar*, without any Ensigns.

Bulbhudur Singh, for the defence of the Doon. About five miles from Dehra was a hill five or six hundred feet high, surmounted with a fort of no great size or strength, called Nalapanee. Here Bulbhudur resolved to make his stand: and employed himself in strengthening and adding to the works, which were still in an unfinished state, when General Gillespie appeared in the neighbourhood.

Misled, in some degree, by his information as to the strength of the place, which had been collected before Bulbhudur had put in hand his recent additions, the Major-General first sent on Colonel Mawbey, with a detachment, to expel the garrison, intending to march immediately with his main body on Nahn. Colonel Mawbey, however, seeing the nature of the works, was deterred from attempting any thing, and solicited fresh instructions. Upon this, the General himself advanced with his whole army; and, after a rapid reconnoissance, resolved on carrying Nalapanee by assault.

On the 30th of October he seized, with a part of his force, one end of the table-land, or rather ridge, which, being more than half a mile in length, was not fully occupied by the fort. Here he formed a hasty battery at six hundred yards for his light guns, intending to try the assault next day. In the course of the night he disposed his division in four parties, which, upon a given signal, were to move simultaneously from the battery and surrounding valleys, with ladders, to escalade the walls. Unfortunately, the signal to be given was the firing of guns in a particular manner from the battery; a method of communication at all times open to accident, and particularly uncertain in a rugged country like that in which Nalapanee was situated, where the columns were necessarily out of sight of the battery; and some of them so far off, that the report could not be heard distinctly.

The Major-General also gave the officers commanding each column reason to expect the signal after ten o'clock in the day; but having early in the morning fired for some time on the walls, without producing so much effect as he expected, the impetuosity of his temper led him to give the signal an hour before the time. Hence it was only obeyed, when given, by two of the four columns, those led by Colonel Carpenter, and Major Ludlow; the former six hundred and eleven strong, and the latter, nine hundred and thirty-nine; officers included. Captain Bulbhudur had made the best possible preparations for defence; besides manning the walls, he opened the wicket gate, which jutted out so as to enfilade a great part of the wall, then barring the entrance with cross beams, he planted a gun through the embrasure thus formed, and loaded it with grape.

The columns approached steadily under a heavy fire of musquetry from the walls, but ignorant of this arrangement to take them in flank. Lieutenant Ellis led his pioneers close under the wall, where they planted the ladders. He was, however, killed immediately after, by the fire of the gun before mentioned; and the greater part of the pioneers, and of the head of the column, were swept down with him.

An attempt was then made to gain the wicket, but without effect; whereupon the troops, finding it impossible to enter the place, fell back to the shelter of some huts, at a little distance outside the walls. The Major-General had stayed this while in the battery; but immediately he saw the troops retire, he hastened forward with three fresh companies of the 53rd, determined to carry the fort or perish. General Gillespie attempted to lead the columns again to the ramparts; but as the men saw no practicable means of surmounting the wall, he was not so readily followed as he wished. He pushed forward, however, with about a hundred dismounted men of the 8th Dragoons; a regiment he had once commanded, and which was much attached to him.

These he led on to within a few yards of the wicket, where, as he was waving his hat, close under the wall, he was shot through the heart, and fell dead. His aide-de-camp, Major O'Hara, was killed by his side; Captain Byers, his brigade-major, was wounded; and of the men of the 8th Dragoons, four were killed, and fifty wounded. The fall of the General was the signal for retreat; and the total loss suffered on this occasion was, besides the General, four officers, and twenty-seven men killed, and fifteen officers and two hundred and thirteen men wounded*.

General Gillespie's death gave the command to Colonel Mawbey of His Majesty's 53rd, the senior officer present. His first act was to retire to Dehra, until a train of heavy guns could arrive from Dehlee, the nearest depot. This occupied till the 24th of November; and on the 25th, the army recommenced operations. A battery of 18-pounders was now constructed, within three hundred yards; and by noon of the 27th of November, a large part of the wall was brought down. A sally was attempted from the fort, but the enemy were driven back by grape from the battery; and the breach appearing to be practicable, an assault was ordered

---

* **Killed**—Lieut, and Adjut. O'Hara, 6th Native Infantry; Lieut, and Adjut. Gosling, Light Battalion; Ensign Fothergill, 17th Native Infantry; Ensign Ellis, Pioneers. **Wounded**—Lieut.-Col. Westenra, slightly; Capt. Brutton, severely; Lieut. Heyraan, slightly; Lieut. Taylor, severely; Cornet Macdonald, severely, 8th Light Dragoons.— Lieut. Young and Lieut. Anstice, severely, his Majesty's 53rd.—Ensign Davidson, slightly, 7th Native Infantry.— Lieut. Broughton, dangerously, 19th Native Infantry.— Major Wilson, and Lieut. Thackeray, severely; Lieut. Monteath, slightly, Light Battalion.—Lieut. Elliott, Pioneers, severely; Lieut. Blane, Engineers, slightly; Capt. Byers, Aide-de-camp, severely. Mr. William Fraser, of the Civil Service, the Political Agent with this division, was also wounded on this occasion, by an arrow, in his throat.

the same day. On approaching the breach, some few of the grenadiers of the 53rd mounted it; but, being immediately shot from within, the rest of the troops hung back, and remained at a short distance, in perfect self-possession, firing at the garrison; but exposed, in return, to the showers of grape, musquetry, arrows, and even stones, which the enemy poured incessantly from behind their defences.

The British officers exerted every effort to induce a second attempt to mount the breach, but without effect. Lieutenant Harrington of the 53rd advanced personally, to prove to the men how easily it was to be ascended; but, being unsupported, he fell a victim to his zeal and gallantry. The British commander, seeing from the battery what was passing, thought it would be of good effect to send up one of his light guns, which, being fired into the breach, might, he conceived, clear it of the enemy, and allow the men to mount in the smoke. Lieutenant Luxford, of the Horse Artillery, undertook this perilous service; but he had no sooner carried up his gun, and executed what was proposed, than he received a mortal wound. The minds of the soldiers were impressed with so superstitious a conviction of the impracticability of the breach, that they would not advance, even with the advantage of the smoke of the gun.

The retreat was, therefore, at last sounded, after two hours had been spent by the assailants in the exposed situation above described, at an immense sacrifice of valuable lives. Four officers, Captain Campbell, 6th N. I.; and Lieutenants Harrington, His Majesty's 53rd, Cunningham, 13th N. I., and Luxford, Horse Artillery, were killed, with fifteen Europeans and eighteen Natives; while seven officers[*], two hundred and fifteen Europeans, and two hundred

---

[*] Major Ingleby, Captain Stone, Lieutenants Horsely, Green, and Brodie, and Ensign Aufrere, of his Majesty's 53rd; and Captain Blake of the 13th Native Infantry.

and twenty-one Natives, were wounded on this occasion. Thus, including the loss incurred in the first attack, this petty fortress had already cost us considerably more than the entire number of its garrison. It was now determined to shell the place, in the hope that from the want of bomb-proofs, or other protection from this arm, it might be made untenable.

The efforts of the besiegers were also directed against the water, which there was reason to believe was got from without the walls. After three days the wisdom of this plan was shown by the evacuation of the fort; which was left by the remnant of its garrison on the night of the 30th of November. It is truly mortifying to reflect, that the same plan, if adopted at the commencement, must have secured the fall of the place with the same facility; and would thus have saved to the nation all the blood that was spilt, besides the loss of two months of the favourable season, and the disrepute of two disastrous failures.

Bulbhudur carried off seventy survivors, all that remained unhurt of his garrison of near six hundred. With these he secretly passed the line of posts established round the fort, and joined a party of about three hundred, which had been sent from Nahn to reinforce the place. They had been seen for some days hovering about the neighbouring hills, but it had not been thought necessary to send a detachment after them. Colonel Mawbey, disappointed that the garrison should escape after all, resolved on an effort to surprise Bulbhudur. He proposed the enterprise to Major Ludlow, who undertook it with alacrity. Having marched the greater part of the night of the 1st of December, the Major came by surprise upon the Goorkha bivouack; it dispersed so quickly that only the advance party were in sight of the enemy; but a number were cut up, and the pursuit was continued for some distance.

Captain Bucke, who commanded the advance, and Ensign Richmond, his adjutant, were wounded, with about fifteen of the Sepoys.

Nalapanee, when occupied by Colonel Mawbey, was found in a shocking state, full of the mangled remains of men and women killed by the shot and shells of our batteries; a number of wounded were likewise lying about, and the stench was intolerable. Upwards of ninety bodies were collected and burnt; and the wounded were sent to our hospitals; after which the fort was razed, and Colonel Mawbey proceeded to execute the further operations assigned to the division.

Experience having shown the determined bravery with which we must expect to be opposed, Lord Hastings so far varied his plan of operations as to forego the detachment of a part of this division to occupy Gurhwal. He accordingly instructed Colonel Mawbey to leave a few men in a strong position for the occupation of the Doon, and to carry his undivided army against Umur Singh's son, Colonel Runjoor Singh Thapa, who was, with about two thousand three hundred elite of the Goorkha army, at Nahn. It was further intended to reinforce the division considerably; and Colonel Mawbey was informed that the command had been conferred on Major-General Martindell. This officer was at a distance, and did not join till the 20th of December.

In the mean time Colonel Mawbey had led back the division through the Keree pass, leaving Colonel Carpenter posted at Kalsee, at the north-western extremity of the Doon. This station commanded the passes of the Jumna, on the main line of communication between the western and eastern portions of the Goorkha territory, and thus was well chosen for procuring intelligence. The letters to and from Umur Singh and his officers, which developed every secret motive of the Goorkha policy, were chiefly intercepted at this point; and after a short time, the disaffection of the inhabitants, and want of supplies, obliged the Goorkhas to abandon Burat, an elevated and strong position north-east of Kalsee; which, being likewise occupied by Colonel Carpenter, entirely cut off Umur Singh's communication with Kumaon and Katmandoo, except by the very difficult routes close under the snowy range.

The division left the Doon on the 5th of December, and taking the route of the plains, entered the valley below Nahn, by the pass of Kolapanee, and encamped at Moganund on the 19th. Nahn was only seven miles distant, and though upon a hill two thousand feet high, was not deemed by the enemy to be of sufficient strength for their main stand. Accordingly Runjoor Singh had received Umur Singh's orders to retire to a position north of the town, and to occupy the surrounding heights and the fort of Jythuk, situated at a point where two spurs of mountainous ridges meet, and the peak at the intersection rises to a height of three thousand six hundred feet above the level of the plains of Hindoostan.

General Martindell having ascertained the evacuation of Nahn, caused it to be occupied by Major Ludlow on the 24th of December; and following with his whole force on the 25th, planned an offensive movement against Jythuk, after a cursory examination of the position as it towered to the skies, and exhibited its several peaks to the view from Nahn.

Two detachments were formed to occupy different arms of the ridges above described. Major Richards, of the 13th N. I. was intrusted with one of a strength of seven hundred and thirty-eight men,* which was to make a de-

---

* Major Richards: light company of his Majesty's 53rd; three and a half light companies of Native Infantry; the battalion companies of the 1st Battalion, 13th Native Infantry, and 50 Pioneers.

tour, and establish itself on a height to the north of Jythuk, subsequently called Peacock Hill. Major Ludlow, of the 6th N. I. was intrusted with the command of the other, which was to occupy the southern and nearest arm to Nahn: its strength was a thousand fighting men.* Mountain-guns, on elephants, were attached to each detachment, but the ground was too rugged to allow of their keeping up on the march. The roads, indeed, were mere mountain pathways, difficult of ascent for a single person, without arms, or accoutrements; and scarcely in any part admitting a march of troops otherwise than by single files.

Major Richards, having-farthest to go, set off an hour earlier; but Major Ludlow, who moved at midnight, came first upon the enemy. He fell in with Runjoor Singh's outer picquet at three in the morning, at about a mile's distance from the point to be occupied. The party retired, and the Major's advance-guard pushed up the hill in pursuit, exposed to its irregular fire. At the top of the hill was the village and temple of Jumpta in ruins, where was a second post of the Nepalese which similarly retired.

Major Ludlow pushed on immediately with the grenadier company of the 53rd, in order to seize the point assigned to him; and on reaching it called a halt, until the rest of his detachment should come up and enable him to secure himself. There was, however, a stockade a little further on, and the grenadiers, mistaking for pusillanimity in the enemy the easy acquisition they had made of several defensible points, thought to redeem the credit that had been lost before Nalapanee, and crowding round the Major entreated to be allowed to storm the post. The impulse of the troops was in unison with the natural ardour of the

---

* Major Ludlow: grenadier company of his Majesty's 53rd, three and a half light companies Native Infantry, nine companies of the 1st bat. 6th Native Infantry, and fifty pioneers.

commander, and he gave way at the sacrifice of his better judgment. He saw, indeed, that the stockade itself was of no great strength, and he thought it might be carried by a *coup-de-main* before the Nepalese should have time to reinforce its garrison. The occurrences at Nalapanee ought to have suggested greater caution.

Juspao Thapa, Runjoor Singh's best officer, was the Goorkha commandant here; and the greater part of the force at Jythuk had, on the first alarm, been collected within or behind the stockade out of sight of the assailants. Juspao allowed the British to come close under the stockade, and then from either side, a little down the ridge, he pushed out parties round both flanks, who opened a fire on the grenadiers from all quarters at once. Not having expected such a reception, the men were confounded, and drew back; whereupon the Goorkhas, seizing the opportunity, charged them sword in hand from the stockade, and, in the end, drove the detachment from all the ground it had gained, in spite of three efforts of Major Ludlow to rally his men. On coming to the Jumpta temple, the Major found his main body of Native Infantry still unformed, and standing confusedly, in a state to afford no support. Indeed, the Sepahees, on seeing the Europeans giving way before the enemy, were panic-struck, and could be brought to no order by the few officers that remained with them. The retreat to Nahn after this was a perfect flight, in which we suffered severely; and so quickly did it pass, that the detachment had returned to camp by ten o'clock in the day; having lost thirty-one Europeans and about one hundred and twenty natives killed and wounded. Lieutenant Munt, 1st N. I. was amongst the former, and there were three officers* in the latter return.

Major Richards had a detour of sixteen miles to make

---

* Lieutenant Scott, 5th; Lieutenant Donnelly, 27th; Lieutenant Sayer, 6th N. I.

before he could reach the post assigned to him, to the north. It was eight in the morning, therefore, before he came to the foot of the ridge on which he was to establish himself. Finding water, he halted till ten, to allow the men to refresh themselves after the march; then continuing his advance, he came on the enemy's first picquet at about a mile from Jythuk, and, following as it retired, took possession of all the ridge to Peacock Hill, within eight hundred yards of the fort. The water of the position was three hundred yards below in a hollow to the left, which rendered a separate post there necessary. The defensive arrangements were complete by noon; but the troops were astonished to hear nothing in the direction of Major Ludlow's post; where, indeed, every thing was over some time before Major Richards arrived at his ground.

While the troops were speculating on this subject, Runjoor Singh's drums beat to arms; and at about one o'clock he paraded his whole force under the walls of Jythuk, preparatory to an attack. The mountaineers advanced boldly at first, but not being able to face a steady volley, they separated; and availing themselves with wonderful dexterity of every jutting rock or the like that afforded cover, kept up a continued irregular fire, charging every now and then when there was any advantage to gain. The ground was, for the most part, too rugged to allow of a charge to dislodge these isolated parties, consequently, during the whole day, our troops had to abide this method of attack without having any cover to shelter them.

At four p. m. Major Richards, fearing that his ammunition would not last, for the bullocks and hill-porters* with the spare rounds had not come up, wrote to Major-General

---

* These were under an escort of the rear-guard, which had separated from the column in the dark of the night, and, losing its way, was observed and cut off by a party from one of Runjoor Singh's stockades.

Martindell to solicit a reinforcement. At the same time, as the Goorkhas were beginning to be more bold and troublesome, he concentrated his force, and gave up the post at the watering-place. By sunset nine charges had been made by the enemy, and repulsed each time by a volley; but as it became necessary to husband the ammunition, the pioneers were employed in collecting stones, which the position was steep enough to render an effectual weapon of defence.

Thus was the post maintained till half-past seven, two hours after sunset, when a positive order arrived from the Major-General to retire. Major Richards had not by this time lost more than twenty or thirty men; but having now no hope of a reinforcement, or of fresh ammunition, he had no choice but to obey. He made, therefore, the best dispositions for retreat that his circumstances would admit; but as there was only a single narrow pathway for the troops to file down, and that skirted sometimes the most tremendous precipices, so as to require careful footing, confusion and loss would have been inevitable, had it been broad day: by night it was, of course, much worse.

The important duty of covering the retreat was undertaken by Lieutenant Thackeray, with his light company belonging to the 26th N. I. This officer's self-devotion contributed mainly to save the detachment from being entirely cut off; for while the troops were filing down the pathway, his company kept the whole Goorkha force in check, charging them several times in different directions. Its situation, of course, grew every instant more desperate, still not a man of the company thought of his individual safety while the Lieutenant lived to command.

After more than half of his men had fallen, he was himself at last killed; and Ensign Wilson, who served under him, fell nearly at the same time. The covering party was then overpowered, and it was supposed at first that the company had been cut off to a man; but it was found afterwards that Runjoor Singh had given quarter to about forty men and a *soobadar*, whom he treated well, and, having vainly tempted to enlist in his ranks, dismissed a few days after on parole not to serve again during the war. Every thing was in confusion in the rear after Lieutenant Thackeray's fall; but most of the troops had filed down the pathway while he was engaged, so that the loss, on the whole, after the stragglers had come in, was three officers killed,* five wounded; and of the men, seventy-eight under the former, and about two hundred and twenty under the latter return. The number of missing, whose fate was for some days uncertain, greatly swelled the first returns; and six officers were amongst these; but the last, Lieutenant Turner, came in on the 1st January, three days after, having had several hair-breadth escapes.

The disasters of this day were owing solely to the irretrievable error of Major Ludlow, in allowing himself to attempt the stockade before he had formed his men, and established the post he was ordered to occupy. Had he first secured his footing on the ridge, those who were driven back would have found a point to rally upon, and the attempt at a *coup-de-main*, whether successful or not, would have been of no consequence. It must, at the same time, be acknowledged that had the native troops been sufficiently officered, it would have been easy to have made head at the Jumpta temple; and it was natural for Major Ludlow to conclude that he would have found his main body ready formed there to support him; but the fault of the system, and the casualties of the war, had unfortunately so thinned the ranks of officers,** that the nine companies of the 1st bat. 6th N. I.

*Killed: Lieutenant Thackeray, 2-26th Native Infantry; Ensign Wilson, 2-26th Native Infantry; Ensign Stalkart, 1-13th Native Infantry.
** Thirty officers had been killed and wounded in the operations before Nalapanee alone.

had no more than three on duty, and this deficiency was the principal cause of the disastrous event on this side.

The prudence and good conduct of Major Richards in the occupation and defence of his position, produced one most advantageous result, as it fully convinced the troops of this division of their great superiority over the enemy in a fair combat. Every man of the detachment felt that had the post been reinforced, or even furnished with fresh ammunition, it might easily have been maintained. Hence the loss was attributed to its proper cause, and the effect of the day's struggle was not diminished by the subsequent retreat. Still, however, something more decisive was wanting to restore complete confidence; and many circumstances contributed at this particular juncture to lead to an exaggerated estimate of the military character of the Goorkha nation.

Thus closed the year 1814 upon this division. No active enterprize was for some time afterwards attempted by Major-General Martindell; but, before relating the operations in which the rest of the season was consumed by him, it may be as well to show what was passing in other quarters, which had similarly become the scene of war.

Chapter 2

Battles & Setbacks

General Ochterlony, who took the field at the same time with Gillespie, and was opposed to Umur Singh in person, formed from the first a just estimate of the character of his enemy, and of the difficulties he would have to encounter. He resolved, therefore, to proceed with the utmost caution. On the 31st of October, the day of Gillespie's fall, he reached Plaseea, situated in a valley within the hills, which he entered from the Sutlej, by a pass less difficult than most of those further east. Umur Singh was at this time at Urkee, considerably within the hills. They run here in broken ridges, stretching N.N.W.; and each ridge affords, of course, a series of positions. The outermost ridge was surmounted by the fort of Nalagurh, which, with an outpost at Taragurh, commanded the principal route into the hills. On the next range stood Ramgurh, Joorjooree, Chamba, and a second Taragurh; above this again, towered the heights of Maloun; behind which, lay Urkee on one side, and on the other the capital of Umur Singh's staunch ally the Raja of Belaspoor. Between, was a comparatively fruitful valley, whence Umur Singh could draw his supplies in case of his occupying any of the above ridges.

Having thrown garrisons into the forts of the Nalagurh and Ramgurh hills, and reckoning, apparently, that General Ochterlony would be occupied some time before them, Umur Singh was in no hurry to leave his position at Urkee. The British General, resolving to put nothing to hazard, made a road with great labour, and sat himself down, with his heavy guns, before Nalagurh on the 1st of November. Having breached the wall, the garrison surrendered on the 5th, capitulating also for the stockade on the same ridge, called Taragurh. Umur Singh came down, and took position on the Ramgurh range the same day, leaving small garrisons at Urkee and Sabathoo behind him.

Having established depots at the captured forts, Major-General Ochterlony proceeded, on the 13th of November, against the Ramgurh positions, sending on Colonel Thompson with a brigade one day's march in advance. The position of Ramgurh was so steep on the side towards the plains, that the Major-General determined to turn it if possible, and operate on its rear. These ridges, it must be observed, are all so many steps to the Heemachul; each, therefore, as it approximates to that stupendous range, towers over that before it, and as you look from the plains, the steeper side is always opposed to you.

Ramgurh stood nearly in the middle of the ridge, and formed Umur Singh's right. Major-General Ochterlony, in advancing from Nalagurh, turned his left; and in the course of November had seized a point from which he hoped to be able to batter one of the stockades of that wing. By the 26th of November, after immense labour in making roads and dragging up the guns, a battery was constructed for 6-pounders; but when it began to play, the stockade was found to be so distant, and so much the higher of the two, that the shot had little effect.

Lieutenant Lawtie, the engineer, seeing this, advanced with a small party to reconnoitre another point a little further on. The Goorkhas, however, sallied out to prevent this, and obliged him to seek the shelter of an old wall that stood near. His critical situation being observed, Lieutenant Williams was sent with two companies from the battery to support the reconnoissance; but a much stronger body came down to the Goorkhas and surrounded the whole party; who thus found themselves under the necessity of cutting their way through the enemy, to secure their retreat*. The manoeuvre was successfully executed; but with the loss of Lieutenant Williams, who was killed, besides seventy-five Sepoys killed and wounded. This affair was of no manner of consequence, except as it afforded to the enemy an occasion of triumph. Next day the Goorkhas gave permission to remove and bury the dead,—a courtesy they never refused during the war, and not the only one we experienced at their hands. General Ochterlony was busily employed all this while in surveying and improving the roads, and reconnoitering Umur Singh's position on every side.

By the 2nd of December he was enabled to form a plan of attack, the object of which was to make a lodgment on a point within the position. The advance was to be made from the battery above mentioned, and was extremely hazardous; inasmuch as there was but one road to the point, and that led under fire of one of Umur Singh's principal stockades, which the advancing column would have to receive on its flank, and perhaps to abide a sally from the

---

* The author of the Military Sketches of the Goorka War gives a different account of this affair. He says that Lieutenant Lawtie, in the course of his reconnoissance, came suddenly on a post, which he deemed it safer to attack than to retreat from. He carried it; but the Goorkhas being reinforced turned upon him; and his Sepoys, after firing away the upper layer of their cartridges, abandoned the post and fled- Lieutenant Williams, who was moving to the support, was, he states, similarly abandoned by his men, who were panic-struck, and fled without exerting themselves. The account given in the text was prepared from official records, before the work here cited was published. The latter will be better authority.

garrison as it passed. However, seeing no other way of seriously annoying the enemy, the Major-General submitted the plan to his two Brigadiers, Colonels Arnold and Thompson, in order to learn their opinion of it.

The propriety of making the attack was still under deliberation, when news arrived of the second failure before Nalapanee; and General Ochterlony also heard of a reinforcement being on its way to his own army, by order of Lord Hastings, which determined him to abandon the plan, and thenceforth to put nothing to hazard. The Major-General had at this time serious doubts of our ultimate success in the struggle, and he feared that our native army, with all its discipline, would be found ill adapted to warfare in a country too rugged to admit of its superior tactics being brought to play. These apprehensions were, however, expressed to none but his Commander-in-Chief; nor could his most familiar associates detect in his demeanour the slightest interruption of that cheerful flow of spirits by which Sir D. Ochterlony has been characterized through life.

While waiting the arrival of the promised reinforcement, Major-General Ochterlony exerted himself in winning over the Plaseea Raja,* and having succeeded in this object, he got him to lend his exertions in making a road for artillery from Mukran, by Khundnee, to Nehur, three miles N.N.E. of Ramgurh, where he had for some time fixed his head-quarters. This was preparatory to an attempt to carry some points in Umur Singh's rear. On the 27th of December, the 2nd bat. 7th N. I., with an additional train of light guns, having joined, Colonel Thompson was detached, with fourteen strong companies, two guns, and two howitzers, to attack two stock-

---

* Raja Ram Surwa Sen was at this time Raja of Hindor and Plaseea.

ades which were opposed to General Ochterlony's right, and were situated on a kind of spur from the Ramgurh ridge, projecting north-eastwards in Umur Singh's rear. The stockades were, if possible, to be carried, and a third point, on which there was no stockade, was then to be occupied by the detachment. Colonel Thompson set off in the night, and late in the morning came opposite the first stockade; but on reconnoitering, thought it not safe to try a *coup-de-main*. He passed on, therefore, in order to seize a ridge about seven hundred yards distant from a stone redoubt belonging to the enemy, and which led to within five hundred yards of Deboo-ka Tibia, the second stockade to be attacked. Here he waited for his guns, and on their arrival fired at Deboo till night, in the hope of effecting a breach.

The Goorkha defences are generally proof against light artillery; hence, no impression being made, Colonel Thompson was compelled to be satisfied with establishing himself on the ridge. In the course of the night the Goorkhas evacuated Deboo-ka Tibia, which Colonel Thompson discovering, sent a party to occupy. The Goorkhas further employed the night in concentrating their force, preparatory to a strong effort to dislodge the detachment. Just before daybreak they commenced a serious attack from a stockade called Mungoo-ka Dhar, which crowned the heights of the Ramgurh ridge, at the point where it was joined by that on which Deboo was situated. The detachment was well on its guard, and drove back the Goorkhas after a few vollies, with a loss of near one hundred and fifty men, whereof sixty were counted on the ground. We had twelve, killed, and fifty-seven wounded, but no officer was of the number.

General Ochterlony, on hearing the firing, sent the 2nd bat. 7th N. I. to reinforce the post; and in the course of the 29th of December, it was stockaded afresh, and otherwise secured. It has been mentioned that Ramgurh formed Umur Singh's right as his position fronted the plains. Colonel Thompson's present post was in the rear of his centre, so as entirely to intercept the supplies he received by the Urkee road, and to incommode the communication with Belaspoor.

Seeing this, the Goorkha General shifted his ground, deserted all his stockades to the left of Ramgurh, and keeping that fort still as his right, took up a reversed position on the other side of it, so as to oppose a new front to our army, which had turned his left. Umur Singh likewise strengthened Mungoo-ka Dhar, and made it his head-quarters. It was soon found that the ridge on which Colonel Thompson was lodged did not afford any means of approaching the main stockades of the enemy's new position, the intervening ground being particularly rugged.

It hence became necessary to devise a different plan of operations, and on the 16th of January, General Ochterlony, still seeking the means of straitening the enemy's supplies, which, since the occupation of the Urkee and Subathoo roads, had been drawn wholly from Belaspoor, put in execution the following masterly movement:—Crossing the Gumba river from Nehur, north-east of Ramgurh, he went along the Urkee road, till he turned the Maloun ridge, and thence, sending on Colonel Thompson ahead, made a long detour in the direction of Belaspoor.

By the 18th of January a party of irregulars, under Captain Ross, occupied the heights of Punalee, commanding Belaspoor, and the valley of the Sutlej, in which it is situated. Colonel Thompson was at the same time a *kos* beyond Jynugur, on the road to the same place, and General Ochterlony himself about to join him. Thus Belaspoor was open; and the power of operating against the north-east face of Maloun, from the valley of the Gumrora, gained. At the same time that this movement was made, Colonel Arnold was left at Deboo-ka Tibia, to watch Umur Singh; and, as it was expected that he would not quietly wait the result, the Colonel had instructions to be on the look-out for a move; and, if the Goorkha army likewise took the route of Belaspoor, to occupy the stockades that would be abandoned, and follow at its heels by a road that would place the enemy between the two British divisions, each of which was more than a match for his whole force.

If the Goorkhas merely retired to Maloun, leaving garrisons in the Ramgurh stockades, Mungoo was to be first proceeded against, in order to maintain the direct communication with the plains and other divisions; and as soon as that point was gained, the brigadier was to advance to Belaspoor. General Ochterlony left his heavy guns with a battalion at Nehur, to be made available in the reduction of Mungoo, and eventually of the Ramgurh forts likewise, after Colonel Arnold should have proceeded to his ulterior destination.

As was expected, Umur Singh no sooner saw the object of the detour made by the head-quarters of the British army, than he moved off with his whole force to take up the stronger position of Maloun, which he feared the British might else preoccupy.

Thus Mungoo-ka Dhar was abandoned and occupied by Colonel Arnold on the 18th January; but small Goorkha garrisons were still left in the stone redoubts of Ramgurh, Taragurh, Chamba, and Joorjooree. Against these Colonel Cooper commenced operations, while Colonel Arnold proceeded, according to his instructions, towards Belaspoor. The latter officer marched along the Ramgurh ridge and under the walls of the remaining Goorkha forts, without experiencing any obstruction from the garrisons.

The movement, nevertheless, took up several days, which were passed in much anxiety and hardship; for, besides the extreme ruggedness of the pathway, the progress of the division was further delayed by a week's heavy rain and snow. It was not, therefore, till the beginning of February, that the brigadier reached Tulsoora, the point assigned to him, and established himself at the extremity of the Maloun range; subsequently he reduced Rutungurh—a fort disjointed from the ridge, but lying directly between Maloun and Belaspoor.

Some time was consumed in reducing the Ramgurh forts; and, during the interval, General Ochterlony employed himself in bringing over the Raja of Belaspoor, who, after an unsuccessful attempt to dislodge Captain Ross from the Punalee heights, had fled across the Sutlej. This Raja, though connected with Umur Singh's family by a recent marriage, was induced at last, through fear of seeing his capital and country given over to another, to make his terms and submit.

Here we shall leave this division for the present, in order to bring on the operations in the Turaees of Gourukpoor and Buhar. Umur Singh had fully justified the reputation he enjoyed as a soldier, by the manner in which he met, and sometimes defeated, the sagacious plans of the British commander. Nothing decisive, indeed, had yet been done by either army; but, considering that the British had been reinforced to near seven thousand men, while Umur Singh had never more than two thousand eight hundred, or at the most three thousand, this was the best possible proof of the skill with which he had availed himself of the advantage of ground, which was all he had to compensate for his numerical inferiority.

The division assembled at Gourukpoor was ordered to take the field on the 15th November; but, owing to the difficulty of collecting hill-porters for the carriage of the baggage and supplies in sufficient abundance in that thinly-peopled district, it was late in December before Major-General J. S. Wood proceeded into the Turaee.

Having waited some time to collect information as to the best mode of penetrating to Palpa, he came at first to the determination of leaving Bootwul to the right, and attacking Nyakot, a post which crowns the hills to the west of the town. Having ascertained, however, that the Goorkhas, under Colonel Wuzeer Singh, a nephew of Bheem Sein's, had taken post at the mouth of the pass, within which Bootwul is situated, and had built there a stockade called Jeetgurh, it was resolved to reconnoitre the works, and carry them, if possible, before proceeding further.

On the 3rd of January, General Wood marched from his camp at Simra, in the Turaee, with twenty-one companies of infantry to put this plan in execution. He acted on the information of a Brahmin, in the employ of the family of the old Palpa Raja, residing at Gourukpoor, and the Brahmin offered his services as guide. The road ran along the banks of the Tenavee, which here is likewise called Goonghee, and the last seven miles of the way led through the Sal forest; but General Wood had been told to expect an open space immediately about the stockade. He was himself, with the advanced guard, still in the thick of the forest, when the road brought them suddenly in front of the stockade, at not more than fifty yards distance.

A smart and destructive fire was immediately opened on the advanced party, and the General's Brigade-Major, Captain Hiatt, and subsequently his engineer officer, Lieutenant Morrieson, were wounded, the latter mortally. This loss was sustained in attempting to reconnoitre the post, preparatory to the advance of the main column, which was headed by His Majesty's 17th regiment, under Colonel Hardyman. Immediately on its arrival, the colonel formed his men, and advanced against the stockade, driving in the party of the enemy who had sallied out on the advance guard; Captain Croker, who led the grenadiers, followed the enemy up the hill, and succeeded in ascending with his own, and two other companies of the regiment, round the left flank of the enemy's work.

Thus a position was gained that commanded it entirely, for it was merely a hollow stockade, running along the declivity. The carrying of the work was therefore certain, indeed the enemy were already retreating from it up the hill behind. General Wood, however, thinking it was not possible to carry the hill also, while, without doing so, the stockade itself seemed to him to be untenable and of no value, ordered a retreat to be sounded, to the great disappointment of the troops, who were flushed with the prospect of a certain and easy victory. The British loss was twenty-four killed, and one hundred and four wounded; besides the two staff-officers above mentioned, Captain M'Dowell, of the artillery, and Lieutenants Pointz and Pickering, of His Majesty's 17th, were severely wounded. The enemy lost a *sirdar*, named Sooruj Thapa, and many more men than we did; but the retreat gave to them the triumph of a decided victory.

The result of this action, and the bravery the enemy had displayed, left in the general's mind an impression of the inadequacy of his force to the objects assigned to it, which influenced all his future measures; instead of endeavouring to penetrate the hills, he confined his operations to defensive precautions. At his solicitation, parties of irregular horse were added to the force; and, in the end, the 8th Native Cavalry was sent to assist in scouring the country, and repelling the enemy's incursions.

Reports magnified the Goorkha army to twelve thousand men; whereas, their regular troops scarcely reached so many hundred. The Major-General, however, giving credence to these exaggerated statements, threw up works at Lotun, and put a garrison there to defend the direct road to Guuruk-poor, while he himself moved with his main body to repel an incursion into Nichloul. These measures contributed to make the enemy bold, and produced a disastrous alarm in our own subjects, which, indeed, was not altogether un-founded: for scarce a day passed without some village be-ing plundered and burnt by the Goorkhas. The same state of things continued during the whole of January, February, and even March; and though reinforced by another native battalion, and with further artillery, General J. S. Wood still considered himself too weak to act offensively.

What had passed simultaneously on the Sarun frontier, and to the eastward, unfortunately tended to confirm this impression; and it is time now to advert to the operations in that quarter.

Major Bradshaw, the negotiator, remained, during the rains, in military charge of the frontier, and disputed lands of Sumroun, as has before been mentioned. The posts he established were not molested, nor had he much commu-nication of any kind with the Goorkhas until October. By that time, some alarm began to be entertained, at Katman-doo, at the extent of preparation witnessed; wherefore, though determined to concede nothing, they still thought it worth while to attempt to amuse the British government with further negotiation, so as, if possible, to spin out the season of operations in empty discussion.

In the course of November, Chundur Seekur Opadheea came down to the Turaee, and sent information to Major Bradshaw that he had a letter and presents for the Governor-General; wherefore he desired a passport to enable him to carry them to Calcutta. The letter was one of congratulation, in the form usual on the arrival of a new Governor-General, and was written as if there were no matters whatever in dispute between the two governments. Major Bradshaw sent to Chundur Seekur a copy of the proclamation of war, issued the first of the month, and refused to let any one pass, or to receive the Opadheea himself, unless he brought full powers to treat for a pacification. The letter was forwarded to the Governor-General, who confirmed the intimation, and further ordered Chundur Seekur to be desired to return to Katmandoo, or remain on the frontier at his peril.

Notwithstanding this intimation, Chundur Seekur lingered in the Turaee, and attempted to get a passport surreptitiously from the Tirhoot Magistrate, who, he thought, would not be aware of the circumstances. He was still at work on this intrigue, when Major Bradshaw, having heard of General Marley's crossing the Ganges, on his way to the Turaee, resolved to defer active operations no longer, but to attack the Goorkha post of Burhurwa, situated on the right bank of the Bagmuttee, and close on the frontier, preparatory to occupying the whole Turaee for the British government. Accordingly he concentrated his force on the 24th of November; and early in the morning of the 25th, surprised and carried the post; killing the Goorkha commander, Pursuram Thapa, and making prisoner Chundur Seekur Opadheea, with his attendants. Major Bradshaw by this means obtained possession of the Opadheea's instructions, which entered fully into the points at issue between the two governments, and completely showed the object of the deputation to have been merely to gain time.

The Goorkhas were very indignant at the seizure of Chundur Seekur, who, they thought, should have been respected as an ambassador, since he had been deputed as such. They forgot, however, that the reception of the individual, or the sanctioning of his deputation, at least, is the thing that plights the faith of the government to whom an agent is accredited, and that this alone gives a claim to the respect of person enjoyed by the envoy of a hostile power and distinguishes him from a spy. Lieutenant Boileau, who commanded the Major's escort, was wounded in personal conflict with Pursuram Thapa during the affair; and there were, besides, two Sepoys killed, and fourteen wounded. Of the enemy, seventy-five were killed or wounded, and ten soldiers were made prisoners, besides Chundur Seekur's attendants.

The Turaee was immediately evacuated by the Goorkhas, and occupied and annexed, *pro tempore*, by proclamation, to the British possessions. Major Bradshaw then established the following posts for its defence, till General Marley should arrive. Captain Hay, with the head-quarters of the Chumparun light infantry, was posted at Baragurhee; Captain Blackney, with a wing of the 2nd battalion, 22nd Native Infantry, was at Sumunpoor, to the right; while Captain Sibley was stationed, with about five hundred men, at Pursa, on the high road to Hetounda, very considerably to the left of Baragurhee.

General Marley arrived in the Puchroutee Tuppa, with the main army, on the 12th of December. An outpost of Captain Hay's had been driven in on the 7th; and the Goorkhas, though they kept within the cover of the Sal forest, had shown many symptoms of an actively hostile spirit. Some attempts at poisoning the wells and pools were discovered; and their spies were known to be busy, several having been detected in our camps. General Marley formed his army into three divisions, intending himself to attempt the Bicheeakoh and Hetounda pass, with twenty-two hundred men; while Colonel Dick, with about fifteen hundred, took the route of Hureehurpoor, to the eastward;

and Major Roughsedge, with one thousand two hundred and eighty men, moved by the Sukteeduree pass and Joor-jooree, which was between the other two, and in advance of Baragurhee. The remainder of the army was to be prepared to support either division that might need it, and to keep open the communications through the forest, till the arrival of the brigade allotted to this duty, which had not yet assembled.

The month of December was spent in devising this plan, and in collecting information preparatory to its execution. In the mean time, the main army was stationary in the Puchroutee Tuppa; and except that Major Roughsedge was at one time, sent to Janikpoor, to the extreme right, the posts above described remained as before. That of Captain Sibley was twenty miles to the left of the main army, which was encamped behind Baragurhee; Captain Blackney was nearly as far to the right—both without support; and, not-withstanding the length of time that they had occupied the same ground, no substantial works had been thrown up by either officer. This state of things induced the Goorkhas to plan a simultaneous attack on both points.

The main army of the Nepalese was collected at Muk-wanpoor, under Colonel Rundher Singh; but the forest was in the possession of different parties, who were always on the alert. Rundher, having exact intelligence of the positions occupied by Captains Sibley and Black-ney respectively, ordered them both to be attacked on the morning of the 1st of January. Shumsheer Rana com-manded the party sent against Pursa; and Surbjeet Thapa, that which attacked Sumunpoor: both were captains, that is, commandants of independent companies or corps in the Goorkha service, and were of high repute with their nation for bravery and conduct.

Captain Blackney was taken completely by surprise

by Surbjeet, who came upon him before daybreak of the new year. Himself, and his second in command, Lieutenant Duncan, were killed in the first onset; and, before the action had lasted ten minutes, the sepoys, who had but partially run to their arms on the alarm, broke, and fled in every direction. To increase the confusion, the Goorkhas set fire to the tents, having penetrated to the heart of the camp before resistance was offered. Lieut. Strettell, the only surviving officer, seeing things in this state, and perceiving that the day was quite irrecoverable, himself joined the fugitives, and retreated to Gora Suhun with the remnant of the detachment. The communication with Captain Hay had previously been cut off, so that it was not possible to retire on Baragurhee.

Captain Sibley was better on his guard at Pursa, where many circumstances had led him to expect an attack. He had, indeed, only recently stated his apprehensions to General Marley, who, on the 31st of December, 1814, sent him a reinforcement under Major Greenstreet. The post was more than twenty miles distant, as before mentioned; and the detachment, having marched in the evening, unfortunately encamped on the road. On the morning of the new year, however, hearing the report of artillery in the direction of Pursa, the Major hastened his march, and got within three miles before the firing had ceased.

The coming-in of the fugitives then sufficiently explained how the affair had ended. It seems that Shumsheer Rana came to the attack in three columns; Captain Sibley's advance had been thrown very considerably forward, and the ground of the position lay between two *nullas*, the windings of which allowed the enemy to penetrate sufficiently on either flank, to cut off the communication between the front and rear. The latter quarter, moreover, was left to the defence of about seventy irregular horse,

59

and was therefore a weak point, especially in a night affair. The attack commenced in front, where it was checked by the advance-guard, commanded by Lieutenant Smith. Finding himself pressed, however, this officer sent to ask of Captain Sibley the reinforcement of a light gun, (a one-and-a-half pounder of new construction,) which was with the detachment.

The Captain brought it forward himself; but when it came, the cartridges were found too large for it to be turned properly to account; and in the mean time, the firing having begun in rear and on both flanks, Captain Sibley found it necessary to return immediately. While on his way back he was wounded, first in the leg, and soon after, mortally, by a shot through the body, from parties of the enemy who had availed themselves of the winding of the *nulla*, to come close in upon the line of communication with the advance. Lieutenant Smith, the next in rank, was immediately summoned from the front to take the command; and, as the firing in the rear was heavy, he judged it right to carry in his advance-guard.

On reaching the line, he found that Shumsheer Rana, while he had thus kept the detachment in play in front and in both flanks, had made his chief attack from the rear; and, having overpowered the irregulars, had penetrated to the officers' tents, and possessed himself of the magazine and *bazar*. The six-pounder, with the detachment, had been turned towards the rear by Lieutenant Matheson, the artillery-officer; and on the junction of Lieutenant Smith with the advance-guard, all that could be done was to form a circle, in order to keep the enemy at a distance. They had established themselves at the magazine, where there were some trees and other cover, from behind which they picked off nearly all the artillery-men. Both Lieutenant Smith and Lieutenant Matheson were sensible that, unless the Goorkhas could be dislodged from this point, the day was lost. On proposing, however, to the sepoys to charge and recover it, they showed a disinclination to the undertaking and kept on firing, nearly at random, until their ammunition was expended.

A retreat was then resolved on; and it was effected by crossing one of the *nullas* at a place where it was not properly fordable, and at a time when the Goorkhas were intent on the plunder. Thus many were saved; but the two guns, the magazine, and stores of every kind, fell a prey to the enemy. Every European of the artillery, except Lieutenant Matheson himself, was either killed or wounded; and our whole loss amounted to one hundred and twenty-three killed, one hundred and eighty-seven wounded, besides seventy-three missing. The detachment originally consisted of about five hundred fighting men; and the proximity of Major Greenstreet, combined with the enemy's eagerness to secure the booty, was what alone saved the wounded and stragglers.

The activity and enterprise shown in these attacks was so unexpected by General Marley, that he began to entertain some apprehension for his train of heavy artillery, which was at the time coming up from Betia, in the rear. Having therefore strengthened the post of Baragurhee, by ordering Major Roughsedge there from Janikpoor, the general himself made a westward movement to cover his train; moreover, considering his force to be insufficient, he abandoned all idea of penetrating the hills in the manner indicated in his instructions. The two brigadiers, Colonels Dick and Chamberlain, agreed with him in representing the army not to be sufficiently strong for offensive measures; and, perhaps, in this respect they were not wrong at the time.

The Marquess of Hastings was seriously disappointed at

all these untoward occurrences. Every nerve was strained to increase the strength of all the divisions, but particularly of this, from which so much was expected. All the military stations of Bengal and Buhar were drained of troops, in order to furnish reinforcements; but it was not so easy to restore confidence to the mind of the commander.

Major-General Marley, notwithstanding the high state of the equipments of his army, and the daily approach of fresh troops, continued inactive during the whole of January; making indeed some marches in the open Turaee, but without once venturing into the forest. Repeated orders came from head-quarters, enjoining some effort at offensive measures.

When, however, the general began to deliberate upon the plan he was to adopt, he was distracted by the different opinions entertained by those he was in the habit of consulting, and came, in the end, to no resolution. In the mean time, the enemy, whose army was at Amowa, burnt several villages at no great distance from his camp, and threatened even to attack Baragurhee, where there were upwards of a thousand men in garrison. They raised a stockade at Soofee, a short distance from the post; and were inspired with such confidence from past successes, that orders were issued, under the red seal, for the attack; but the Goorkha commander, Bhugut Singh, had better information than the council at the capital, and wisely refrained.

The court, however, not satisfied with his reasons, attributed his conduct to cowardice; and summoning him to the capital, to answer for the disobedience, made him appear at the Durbar in woman's attire, as wanting the spirit and courage of a man. They were soon afterwards undeceived; and on the 7th February removed the post they had so impudently established. But to the mortification of the troops, and discredit of the British general, it had continued thus to insult us for near a month with impunity. Major Roughsedge, indeed, a day or two before the evacuation, sent Captain Hay with a party from Baragurhee to reconnoitre, and, if possible, dislodge the enemy; but that officer, finding his approach intercepted by a morass, and seeing that the post was too strong for his detachment to carry by assault, contented himself with firing a few shrapnell shells from a couple of 6-pounders he had with him, and retired again to Baragurhee.

On the 10th February, General Marley, unable longer to endure the irksomeness of his situation, and feeling strongly the impossibility of answering the expectations of his commander-in-chief, took the sudden and extraordinary resolution of leaving the camp, which was then at Bunjaree Pookureea. He set off before daylight in the morning, without publishing any notification of his intention to the troops, and without taking any means of providing for the conduct of the ordinary routine of command during his absence.

The resolution had previously been formed by Lord Hastings of providing another commander for the Sarun army; but the unadvised step into which General Marley was thus betrayed, seemed to him to require his permanent removal from the staff.

Major-General George Wood was ordered up from the presidency to succeed General Marley; and Colonel Dick, the senior brigadier, assumed and continued to exercise the command until his arrival.

We have now brought up the operations of this campaign to the period when the succession of disasters had reached its crisis. General Ochterlony alone had not been foiled. He was steadily pursuing his plan by slow and secure manoeuvres, but had yet gained no brilliant advantage over his equally cautious antagonist.

General Martindell's division had failed three times: twice before Nalapanee, and the third time in the attempt to take up positions before Jythuk. Moreover, the aggregate loss sustained by this division had amounted to a third of the numbers that originally took the field from Meeruth. The army assembled at Gourukpoor had allowed itself to retire before the enemy under circumstances amounting to a repulse; while, as we have seen, the Buhar division, which was thought strong enough to have penetrated to Katmandoo, had lost two detachments of five hundred men each, without an equivalent success of any kind.

From the frontier of Oudh to Rungpoor, our armies were completely held in check on the outside of the forest; while our territory was insulted with impunity, and the most extravagant alarms spread through the country. We had lost nothing, indeed, on the Morung frontier; on the contrary, the cooperation of the Sikhim Raja had been gained, the communication having been opened by an overture on his part, and a request for a few military stores. In this quarter, also, an attempt made by the Goorkha commander in Morung to cut off a post of ours stationed at Moodwanee, had failed; Lieutenant Foord, of the 9th N. I. having repulsed their night attack, after the assailants had succeeded in firing his tents and baggage. We had several killed, and Lieutenant Thomas, of the 9th, was amongst the wounded, in this affair, which was very creditable to the troops and officers; but as the position was next day evacuated, there was little to boast of in the victory.

Major Latter, indeed, was led by the vigorous nature of the attack to solicit the aid of some reinforcements, then on their way to the Sarun army; and thus, by withholding them from their destination, yielded the enemy some advantage from the attack, notwithstanding its failure. The alarms of the civil authorities of Tirhoot had produced a similar diversion in that quarter; and it was not until the end of February, or, indeed, the beginning of March, that the division destined for the main attack was augmented to the full strength proposed for it.

CHAPTER 3

A Turn of the Tide

The uniform success which had hitherto attended the
Goorkhas produced, in January 1815, an effect on the public mind in the independent portion of India which is more
easily imagined than described. Although jealous, naturally, of our preponderance, and suspicious to a degree of
any relinquishment of the pacific policy, the native powers
had so little knowledge of the strength and resources of
the Goorkhas, that the war at first excited little sensation.
It was regarded as a mere affair with a troublesome Raja
of the frontier; and, but for the greater magnitude of our
preparations, might have been assimilated to the measures
taken in 1812 against the Rewa chief.

As one check, however, followed another, speculation
grew more active, and the events of the campaign became
matter of intenser interest; until, at last, more than one of
the native courts began seriously to think it was time to
prepare to take advantage of circumstances. Runjeet Singh,
the Punjab Seikh, kept an army at Lahore, and seemed to
menace us in the extreme north-west; while Ameer Khan
collected together his Putan battalions, and made an am-
biguous offer of their services, from a point only a few
marches from Agra. The tone, moreover, assumed in Sindheea's *durbar* and at Poona was any thing but conciliatory.

It is not our business in this place to explain at length

the attitude assumed by the native powers, in consequence of the altered view of our position presented by these disasters. Suffice it to say, that the intrigues which were set on foot throughout the whole independent portion of India, and which led to such important results a few years afterwards, date their commencement from this period. In proportion as their existence became manifest, it was of course more necessary that we should persevere and conquer the subsisting difficulties in the hills; for the name and character of the government and of the British nation were felt to be committed on the issue.

The Marquess of Hastings never doubted for an instant of his ultimate success in the campaign; and notwithstanding the unfavourable aspect of things at the commencement of 1815, there were abundant sources of consolation, and of a just confidence, to those who looked beyond the surface. Every check our arms had experienced was clearly traceable to a want of due precaution in those who directed the operation, and this was an error that was sure to be remedied as soon as felt. Thus every encounter, even when unfavourable in its result, brought more strength in the lessons of prudence it inculcated, than was detracted in the physical loss sustained.

The soldiers and *sepahees* of the British army had, for some time, been unused to war; but though somewhat open to the influence of panic from the strangeness of the scene, and novelty of their situation amidst the forests and mountains of this extraordinary region, and moreover a little disheartened, at first, to find their best efforts thwarted by this semi-barbarous enemy, they yet showed a wonderful buoyancy of spirit in soon recovering their wonted nerve. The Goorkhas, on the other hand, were abundantly satisfied with repulsing an attack or cutting off an outpost. They never pushed their success beyond this; and were indeed too deficient in military science, as well as in physical means, to assume a superiority in the campaign, or act offensively on a large scale, against any one of our divisions. Their tactics were purely defensive; so much so, that howsoever severely their assailant might suffer from the indiscretion of his first attack, they left him ample time to collect fresh courage, and approach them again with more caution.

To the officers of the Bengal army, in particular, were the lessons of this war salutary; precipitancy and want of caution were qualities bred in them, by an uninterrupted course of easy victory. From the days of Clive to those of Lord Lake, they had only to show themselves, and march straight against their enemy, to ensure his precipitate flight. They naturally carried into the hills the same contempt of the foe which their victories in the plains had engendered; and were taught only by painful experience to make sufficient allowance for the entire change of circumstances in the new field of action. They had, however, to guard against another influence as prejudicial as over confidence; and that was, too great distrust and apprehension after the experience of a check. It is doubtful which extreme was, in its results, most injurious to the British cause: but more than one of the officers in high command afforded an example of the facility with which the mind passes from one to the other, as well as of the obstinacy with which distrust maintains its hold when once it finds admittance.

It must be allowed to the Goorkhas that they were an experienced as well as a brave enemy: they had been continually waging war in the mountains for more than fifty years, and knew well how to turn every thing to the best advantage. Caution and judgment were, therefore, more required against them, than boldness of action or of decision; but most of all, that power of intelligence and discrimination which is never without a resource in circumstances the most unexpected.

It will be perceived that little advance was made in the campaign until we had learnt to turn the same advantages to account against the enemy, by the help of which he foiled us so often at the commencement; for with all the experience of Indian warfare, combined with the professional science of Europe, our officers found yet something to learn from these Goorkhas. We adopted from them the plan of stockading posts, which the nature of the campaign frequently rendered it necessary to place beyond the limit of prompt support. Had this plan been adopted from the first, the detachments of Captains Sibley and Blackney would have been saved. It was, however, altogether a new thing to the Bengal army; for, from the earliest days, there had never been works thrown up for the defence of an outpost; nor in a war of the plains, could there ever be occasion for such a precaution. Sir David Ochterlony has the merit of having first resorted to this plan,* and of having adopted it, too, as a resource of prudence which occurred to his own mind, not taught to him by the experience of disaster, as was the case with others.

Such, however, was the nature of Umur Singh's positions that they could not have been turned or surrounded, so as to cut off his communications without occupying a large circuit, and throwing out detachments for the purpose at considerable distances from one another; many of which, being necessarily much exposed, would have been liable to be overwhelmed separately, but for this simple though substantial defence.

---

* The first stockade erected after the Goorkha fashion was at Khundnee, where a battalion was left with some irregulars, while the division turned Umur Singh's left, by marching to Nehur.

The strength of the stockades was originally greatly miscalculated: made up of rough hewn wood and stones, heaped together between an inner and outer palisade, they were in appearance so contemptible as to invite assault without even seeming to require breaching.

On the plains, much more formidable-looking places were constantly carried in that way: but appearances were deceitful; and the Goorkhas, having a just confidence in their defences, always stood boldly to them, and made the assailants pay dearly for their temerity. The lighter artillery made little or no impression, and the difficulty of bringing up heavy guns, rendered them, in truth, most formidable defences. The wood and materials for raising them were every where at hand, and the celerity with which they could be prepared in any position formed a main source of the strength of the country. But this was a resource equally available to an invader, and one which placed the issue in the power of continuance, that is, in the length of the purse. By the adoption of this system, the operations of the divisions which penetrated the hills were entirely converted into a war of posts, as will have been already sufficiently manifest from the character of General Ochterlony's proceedings.

The same plan was ultimately put in practice at Jythuk, Kumaon, and elsewhere. Its effect will presently be fully shown; but first, it will be proper to mention the result of the efforts made against the more central possessions of the enemy.

The operations of the Sarun and Gourukpoor armies may be dismissed with a very few words. Major-General George Wood was appointed General Marley's successor, and joined the camp on the 20th of February. The very day before his arrival, an event occurred that struck terror into the enemy, and raised the courage of this army to the highest pitch of confidence. Lieutenant Pickersgill, an active officer of the intelligence department, discovered, while out reconnoitering, a party of about five hundred Goorkhas at no great distance from camp. He immediately sent intimation to Colonel Dick, the senior officer, who had assumed the command on General Marley's departure, and himself remained with his personal escort to watch the enemy. Colonel Dick sent a party of irregular horse, under Cornet Hearsey, to strengthen Lieutenant Pickersgill, and himself followed, with all the picquets of the army, in the hope of cutting off this detachment.

The Goorkhas, who had taken an advantageous position in a hollow, finding themselves unmolested by Lieutenant Pickersgill, and seeing his small numbers, came to the resolution of attacking him. Just, however, as they debouched from their position for the purpose, they perceived the cavalry, and the further support that was advancing. Appalled by this, they attempted a precipitate retreat, when Lieutenant Pickersgill, waiting only to be joined by Cornet Hearsey's horse, fell upon them, and cut the whole detachment to pieces. A number of officers of the army had ridden out from camp immediately on its being known that a party of the enemy were in sight, and these joined in the charge, and were mainly instrumental to its success.

The Goorkhas were so intimidated by this result, that they hastily withdrew every position they had established in the forest and Turaee; and when General G. Wood arrived next day, the passage of the forest was free to him— not a Goorkha being to be seen below the hills.

The season was doubtless very far gone for any thing now to be commenced, nevertheless, there remained a month to make some effort to redeem the consequences of his predecessor's inactivity; and the army naturally expected to be led through the forest after the enemy, if not into the passes of the hills. The new General, however, adopted an opinion that the season of the fever had arrived, and that it would be risking the health and efficiency of his fine army, which was now augmented to thirteen thousand four hundred regular troops, were he to attempt to penetrate the forest. He accordingly contented himself with sweeping its skirt, in a long march eastward to Janikpoor and back again; and thus the season closed, actually without his seeing a single enemy.

In Gourukpoor, Major-General John Sullivan Wood burnt a few of the Goorkha villages in retaliation of their excesses, and marched wherever he heard the enemy were advancing. He was, however, still deceived by false reports, and could not get rid of the impression that his force was too weak to effect any thing against Wuzeer Singh, whom he represented to head-quarters as commanding an army numerically much superior to his own. On the necessity of ascertaining this point, by coming actually into contact with the enemy, being strongly urged by the Commander-in-Chief, General Wood was induced at the close of the season, that is, in the month of April, to appear again before Bootwul. He accordingly, on the 17th of that month, drew up his army, and opened a desultory fire against the place for some hours, from his artillery and line.

The manoeuvre produced no result whatever, though attended with several casualties. The General, however, described it as a reconnoissance calculated to create a diversion by alarming the enemy on this frontier, at the same time that it enabled himself to ascertain that he had not miscalculated the strength of the army opposed to him. General Wood immediately after this manoeuvre laid waste the Goorkha portion of the Turaee, and then retired to cantonments at Gourukpoor.

It is fortunate for the interest of this narrative that the

spirit of enterprize was not every where so wanting as in the leaders of the two central divisions. In proceeding westward, it now becomes our duty to relate a series of operations of a very opposite character.

It was ascertained by Lord Hastings, while on his tour through Rohilkhund, that the province of Kumaon, which skirts the north of it, was nearly destitute of troops; the whole Goorkha force having been drawn off to oppose the British divisions operating to the east or west. It seemed to him that a diversion in this quarter, while it would distract the enemy by multiplying the points of attack, would further be of use in preventing any reinforcements from proceeding westward to Jythuk. If successful, it might lead to very important results, even to the conquest of the province, and entire separation of the eastern from the western territory: if the contrary, the effect would be produced in other quarters without much loss. It is to be observed that the Kumaonese were known to be disaffected to the Goorkhas, who held them in rigorous subjection, frequently seizing and selling into servitude their women and children, in order to enforce the most arbitrary exactions. The consequent alienation of the population from their masters, was reckoned upon as likely to aid greatly the projected enterprize.

There were no regular troops that could be spared at this juncture (December); for the threatening tone and position of several chiefs and associations of the south and north-west required that a warlike attitude should be maintained on both frontiers; whilst the demands for reinforcements to the divisions already in the hills, were so urgent as to require every disposeable man. In order, therefore, not to lose the opportunity, Lord Hastings resolved to avail himself of the warlike population of Rohilkhund, who are Putans, of a race trained from infancy to the use of the sword and matchlock, and naturally brave and impetuous, though not easily subjected to discipline. Two officers, used to such troops, were accordingly ordered to make levies of Rohillas, to be employed against Kumaon. The persons selected were Lieutenant-Colonel Gardner, and Major, then Captain, Hearsey, neither of them of the regular establishment, but both Mahratta officers of great merit, who had come over under the proclamation of Lord Wellesley, on war breaking out with Sindheea in 1802-3. Lieutenant-Colonel Gardner had since been retained in command of a corps of police-horse; Major Hearsey had not been employed in a military capacity for some years, but was the companion of Mr. Moorcroft's adventurous journey across the snowy range to the lake Manusararwa, and had been detained in Kumaon as a prisoner, along with Mr. Moorcroft, on their return, the very year before the war broke out.

To the former officer it was assigned to penetrate from Kasheepoor in the Moradabad district; while the latter was to operate against Chumpawut, to the east of the province, by the passes near Peeleebheet and Khyreegurh, where the Deoha, or Gogra, forces its way into the plains. Both officers received their instructions late in December, and proceeded at once to organize levies.

On the 11th of February, 1815, Lieutenant-Colonel Gardner commenced his march from Kasheepoor, accompanied by a civilian, his relation, the Honourable Edward Gardner, to whom was assigned the function of political agent for the province. On the 15th, the force reached the foot of the first passes, and dislodged a Goorkha picquet from Deklee: from hence they could see distinctly a party of Goorkhas stockaded on the summit of Kat-kee-nao, an elevated post which overlooked the entrance of the pass, by the bed of the Kosila; while another party of the enemy occupied the *Gurhee*, or fort of Kotha, considerably to the right. Having reconnoitered the two positions, the Lieutenant-Colonel determined on an attempt to penetrate them, so as, if possible, to get between the garrisons and Almora.

On the 16th, in order to put the above design into execution, the Lieutenant-Colonel made a short march up the Kosila to Chookum, and next day halted: that the same hill porters who attended the advance, might return to bring up the rest of the baggage and supplies. Heavy rain commenced on the 18th, which soon filled the river, and otherwise impeded the advance. In the evening, however, a party was sent in the direction of Kotha, as if to threaten that post; and at the same time two hundred Rohillas, and one hundred Mewatees marched up the river, to endeavour to seize a strong pass, called Thangura, where the Kosila rushes through a defile commanded by lofty and precipitous mountains on either side.

This party, from some misconduct of the guide, did not secure the pass on both sides of the river; but established itself on the hill overlooking it to the south-east. The detachment sent in the direction of Kotha, fell in with the garrison on a hill called Ronseldeh, between the Thangura pass and Kotha. Lieutenant-Colonel Gardner, therefore, deeming it necessary to dislodge the enemy from this post without loss of time, moved next morning with five hundred men for the purpose. The object being effected, he turned towards Thangura, and encamped for the night at Ookul Danga, where his party had established themselves, as above mentioned, on the evening before.

On the 20th, the Goorkhas evacuated Kat-kee-nao, and retired to Googur Gurh, on the right of the Kosila, near Thangura. Kat-kee-nao was immediately secured by a party of observation sent for the purpose the preceding day; and in the evening, the Lieutenant-Colonel in person crossed the river, and dislodged the enemy from Googur; thus securing both sides of the important pass of Thangura. On the 21st, seven hundred Rohilla Putans moved forward to Seethee, where they bivouacked, and were next day pushed on to a point where two roads to Almora meet, at a *peepul* tree. The more open route, by the valley and town of Boojan, was found occupied by the Goorkha Surdar (Rungelee), with the concentrated garrisons of Kotha and Kat-kee-nao.

After a short halt therefore to refresh, the Lieutenant-Colonel marched with all haste to seize the Choumou hill, the first steep ascent on the other road; which, leaving the valley, runs along the ridge to the north or left of the direct line of advance. The whole day was consumed in this arduous march; and at the close of it, there was an ascent of three *kos* to the summit which it was intended to occupy. The fatigue was so great, that only about forty men of the whole number came to the ground; and these were supplied with water from the snow, which lay there in abundance. Early in the morning of the 22nd, the enemy were seen making for the same point: they were led by Ungut Surdar, who had just arrived with a reinforcement from Almora. The party at Choumou were still extremely weak; but they had several standards, of which they made such a display as deterred Ungut from an attack which he seemed to meditate.

It was the 28th of February before all the supplies could be brought up from the rear to Choumou: on that day, however, a further short advance was made to Kampena-ke-danda; whence the enemy were seen in force at Koompoor, a rugged hill in front.

The Lieutenant-Colonel, having been obliged to form depots and establish garrisons at Kat-kee-nao, Kotha, and several other places in his rear, thought it prudent to wait here for further reinforcements; and particularly for one thousand Putans raised at Hapur in the Meeruth district, and now on their way to join him. Little happened in the interim of this halt, with the exception of two skirmishes, on the 6th and 18th of March; both of which ended in a manner highly creditable to the Rohillas. In the former, the Lieutenant-Colonel's advanced-guard succeeded in driving back a party of the enemy who ventured to descend from their stockade into the intervening valley of Tarakot; and in the second affair, which was rather more serious, between six and seven hundred men being engaged on either side, the Putans made a resolute charge, and put to the rout a body of the enemy of equal strength, who ventured again to the same ground.

The Lieutenant-Colonel, while he thus advanced by the Kosila, had kept a party in front of the direct route from Rohilkhund by Bumouree and Bheem Tal; the commandant, however, attempted nothing, and was in the end ordered to join the main body.

Major Hearsey, having completed his levies, at the same time with Colonel Gardner, advanced also, in February, from Peeleebheet, and penetrated by the Kalee, or western Gogra, to Chumpawut, without meeting any opposition. The population showed some disposition to declare in his favour; so, posting half his force to guard the important passes of the Kalee, he began to think of co-operating with Lieutenant-Colonel Gardner, by an advance to Almora from the east.

In this view he moved upon Kootulgurh, a very strong fort; but which some information received as to the state of its supplies, induced the Major to think must soon yield to a blockade. The month of March was spent in these operations.

In the mean time, Colonel Gardner being joined by the

men from Hapur, on the 22nd of March, again out-generaled the Goorkha commander, and established himself in his rear, and even within sight of Almora. The same night that the reinforcement joined, a strong detachment under Mohun Singh, a native commandant of known courage and steadiness, was sent, by a circuitous route through the valleys to the right, to seize the southernmost point of a ridge immediately facing Almora, where was a temple called Sheeo-ka Devee.

On the morning of the 23rd, in order to draw off the enemy's attention from this operation, a demonstration was made of attacking Koornpoor in front. The movement was thus so well concerted, that it was not till twelve o'clock in the day that the Goorkhas made the discovery of its object, by seeing the Rohillas taking up their position at the temple behind them. The Lieutenant-Colonel, satisfied at the success of the operation, waited till the following day to see its effect on the enemy. Early in the morning he advanced with the intention of attacking, or at least turning, the left flank of the Koompoor position, in order to follow to Sheeo-ka Devee.

The Goorkhas, however, moved at the same time; and setting fire to their stockade, hastened by Reonee to Kutarmul, two points on the same ridge with Sheeo-ka Devee. The Lieutenant-Colonel followed by the same route; but the want of porters prevented his reaching Reonee till the 25th, and a halt of a couple of days was then necessary, to bring up the guns and supplies.

On the 28th he marched in two columns upon Rutarmul; and as he approached, the Goorkha commander, finding himself between Mohun Singh's detachment and the main body, did not think it prudent to continue on the same ridge, but crossed the Kosila, and posted himself on the declivities between Almora and that river, leaving the

Lieutenant-Colonel free to occupy the ground on the right bank from Reonee to Sheeo-ka Devee. Thus had Lieutenant-Colonel Gardner, by sheer dexterity, and without bloodshed, made an effectual opening to the heart of the province of Kumaon. His conciliatory conduct, and that of the Political Agent, had succeeded in effectually gaining the natives; so much so, that the *bazar* of his camp seldom failed to be supplied from the villages in the hills; and the intercourse opened and maintained furnished certain intelligence of all the enemy's projects.

In the end of March, Lord Hastings, seeing the state of things here, determined on supporting the Lieutenant-Colonel and following up his successes, by sending a force of regular infantry and artillery, capable of subduing all further opposition. He selected Colonel Jasper Nicolls, at the time Quartermaster-General of the King's troops in India, for this important service; and on the 23rd of March, placed under his command a force of two thousand and twenty-five firelocks, composed of the 1st battalion 4th N. I., under Captain Faithful; the 2nd battalion 5th N. I. under Major Patton; and part of a battalion formed of grenadier companies, and then employed in Gurhwal. Ten pieces of artillery of different kinds were added from Moradabad.

The state of the operations before Jythuk, combined with the assurance that the tranquillity of Central India would not be disturbed this season, were the circumstances that enabled the Governor-General to devote the troops of his regular army to this service now; though two months earlier he had not deemed it safe to spare them.

On the 5th of April, Colonel Nicolls entered the hills with his advance, and hastened to join Lieutenant-Colonel Gardner at Kutarmul. On his way he heard of the entire defeat and capture of Major Hearsey, and of the reduction of all the posts he had established to guard the line of the Kalee or Surjoo; by which names the western branch of the Gogra is here known. It seems that the court of Katmandoo, finding all secure for the season to the eastward, determined on an effort to succour Almora, and eventually relieve Jythuk. For this purpose they ordered a battalion to cross the Kalee into Kumaon, and gave the command of the force to Hustee-dul, the chief then governing the province of Dotee.

Having strengthened himself by collecting all the detachments of his province, this chief crossed the Kalee, on the 31st of March, at Khusmot Ghat. Major Hearsey had attempted the defence of a wider line along this river than his force justified, besides being still engaged on the blockade of Kootulgurh. His men were thus too much detached for his whole force to be made available in the emergency; nevertheless, he hastened to meet the enemy with the few men he had at Chumpawut, and fell in with him on the first day's march. The Rohillas, being raw levies, deserted Major Hearsey after the first fire; and he was wounded, and made prisoner.

None of the positions he had garrisoned held out afterwards; but the men hastened back again to the plains with the utmost terror and expedition. Little better was to be expected from new levies, upon the loss of their commander; the defeat was, however, of bad effect in the impression it left on the inhabitants of the province; and had not the support been on its way to Colonel Gardner, its influence on the raw troops of his force might, perhaps, have rendered necessary the relinquishment of all the advantages gained. It may be observed here, that in every action between the Goorkha regulars and Rohilla Nujeebs, or other similar levies, the former were always victorious. Hence the merit of Colonel Gardner's plan, under which, though always advancing to his object, he avoided committing his men, except in skirmishes where he had a decided superiority, or under circumstances in which the enemy did not think it prudent to attack him, is the more conspicuous.

Colonel Nicolls, on being informed of the defeat and capture of Major Hearsey, hastened to effect a junction with Lieutenant-Colonel Gardner, and reached him a day or two before Hustee-dul arrived with his prisoner at Almora. The latter event was announced by a salute which was both heard and seen from the British camp. On the 23rd of April, Hustee-dul again left the town, with a considerable detachment, upon some expedition, the object of which was not immediately apparent. Colonel Nicolls, seeing the movement, despatched Major Patton, with his battalion, the 2nd of the 5th N. I., in the direction of Gunnanath, a station about fifteen miles north of Almora, on which Hustee-dul appeared to be marching.

The routes of the two detachments brought them in sight, and close upon one another, before they were well aware. They were both marching up the same eminence, and it was a contest which should seize it. Hustee-dul first gained the summit; but the British advance-guard, under Lieutenant Webster, of the 5th N. I., attacked him before he had time to make any arrangement for his defence. He was dislodged with considerable loss; and in the action received a ball in his temple, which secured the victory to us. Our loss was only two killed, and twenty-five wounded, including Ensign Blair, severely.

Hustee-dul was an active and brave officer, of high reputation in his nation, and his loss was severely felt in Almora.

Colonel Nicolls determined, on the return of Major Patton, to avail himself of the alarm he judged the late defeat would occasion; and on the 25th, at one p. m., he led the

1st battalion 4th N. I. in person across the Kosila, followed by Lieutenant-Colonel Gardner and his irregulars, in order to effect a lodgement on the Seetolee heights, where the enemy were posted. Having reached the height and taken measures to secure the possession of it, he thought he observed symptoms of alarm in the garrison of a stone breast-work before him, and immediately in front of the town of Almora.

He was hence tempted to try an assault, without waiting to bring up his guns to breach the walls, which would have occasioned a considerable loss of time. The assault was led by Captain Faithful in person; and the redoubt was entered first, through an embrasure, by Lieutenant Wight, who fell immediately, severely wounded by a Goorkha chief. Captain Faithful followed at the head of some grenadiers, and saved his brother officer by cutting down the man; when the rest fled, leaving the redoubt in our possession. All the stockades of the ridge were carried or evacuated; and the enemy were pursued into the town of Almora; leaving the Colonel to make his dispositions for the night.

The Nepalese were not, however, disposed to resign the possession of these heights, which communicated directly with the town, without a further struggle; and accordingly, at about eleven in the night, having sent a detachment secretly round, they attacked and carried our most northerly post, though stockaded and defended by a piquet of regulars, under Lieutenant. Costly, of the 1st battalion of 4th N. I. A party of the flank battalion, under Lieutenants Brown and Winfield, immediately moved to the support of the post; and with the aid of a *ghole* of irregulars, under Colonel Gardner in person, the place was recovered, but not without a hard struggle.

The firing in this quarter was the signal for a general sortie from the fort; but for this Colonel Nicolls was prepared, and the enemy were driven back with loss; after which they confined themselves to a little detached firing. We lost in this affair an officer, Lieutenant Tapley of the 27th, attached to the grenadier battalion, besides many sepoys and irregulars killed and wounded.* The next day the guns were brought up, and a position taken about seventy yards only from the fort of Almora. Bumsah Chountra, the governor of the province, seeing his situation desperate, proposed in the evening of the following day a suspension of arms, preparatory to a negotiation of the terms of surrender.

The armistice being granted, the Nepalese wounded officers came boldly into our camp to solicit surgical aid. They further stated, without reserve, their extreme want of supplies, and allowed us to examine the walls and defences of the place; thus exhibiting a frankness and confidence not a little remarkable in their circumstances. In arranging the terms of capitulation, their main stand was made to obtain an article permitting five hundred men, destined to the service by the government at Katmandoo, to proceed westward, to reinforce Runjoor Singh at Jythuk. This, of course, was resisted; but they did not give up the point until a renewal of hostilities was threatened, if the surrender were not concluded by a given hour. At last, on the 27th of April, a formal convention was signed by Colonel Nicolls and the Honourable Edward Gardner, on one side, and Chountra Bumsah, Ungut Kajee, and Chamoo Bundaree, on the other.

---

* Including the operations in the day-time, the loss in the attack and maintenance of the Seetolee position, was one officer, Lieutenant Tapley, twenty-nine sepoys, and twenty irregulars killed; two officers (Lieutenants Wight and Purvis, of the 4th native infantry), ninety-eight sepahees, and sixty-one irregulars wounded. Making a total of two hundred and eleven killed and wounded.

In this the surrender of the province of Kumaon, with all its fortified places, was stipulated; also the retirement of all troops and officers of the Goorkha government, within ten days, to the east of the Kalee; the British engaging to furnish carriage to aid the transportation of private property. Major Hearsey's unconditional release was further stipulated. These articles were faithfully executed; and Colonel Nicolls, having accompanied the Goorkha troops to the ghats of the Kalee, disposed his force in the best manner for the defence of that line, against any future attempt of the Nepalese to molest our possession of the province.*

* During the operations above explained, the Goorkhas made an irruption from Dotee into Khyreegurh, in the plains; but were defeated and driven back by a detachment under Captain Buchanan, sent from Futchgurh by Lord Hastings.

CHAPTER 4

Victory in Kumoan

Let us now return to the events of the campaign further west. It has been stated that Major-General Martindell, after the failures of December, was so firmly persuaded of the inadequacy of his force to do any thing against the position of Jythuk, that he lay long inactive at Nahn. In the interim, several reinforcements reached him; and the instructions of his Commander-in-Chief continually urged the recommencement of active operations. Towards the beginning of February, Major Kelly was detached from Nahn, with a light battalion, to occupy a post on the same ridge that Major Ludlow had moved upon in December.

He established himself without opposition at Nounee; and on the 12th of the month, being supported by Major Ludlow and his battalion, he advanced to a point called the Black Hill. This post being within the range of heavy artillery, it was resolved by the Major-General to carry up 18-pounders, and batter the first of the enemy's stockades. The side of the hill was therefore prepared for the purpose, and, by great exertions, guns and stores were dragged up the precipitous part of the ascent. The operation excited the astonishment of the enemy, who came out every where to see the wonder, but made no attempt to prevent it. In the mean time, Runjoor Singh's communications were left quite open; and besides the reinforcement carried to him by Bulbhudur Singh, others were continually joining. On the 17th of February, intelligence reached camp of a party being on its way to Jythuk, from the Jumna. Lieutenant Young was accordingly detached with a body of irregulars to intercept it. Not finding the enemy at the point expected, he came back on the 19th; but more correct intelligence being then obtained, he again marched with all the irregulars in camp, amounting to upwards of two thousand men, and found the Goorkhas in a place called Chumalgurh. Not thinking it right to trust his raw troops with an immediate attack of the position, and relying on his great superiority of number, he proceeded to post detachments where most they could annoy the enemy, and cut off the communication with Jythuk.

The whole number of the Goorkhas did not amount to two hundred fighting men; but seeing their situation desperate, they called a council, and adopted the resolution to die bravely together*. Having thus prepared themselves, they advanced, and delivering their fire, charged, sword in hand, the nearest post of the irregulars. These unfortunately gave way immediately, and were pursued, in the utmost confusion, to the next post, where the panic quickly spread; until the whole party took to flight without attempting any resistance, in spite of the utmost efforts of Lieutenant Young to induce them to face the enemy.

This unlooked-for result of their intrepidity enabled the Goorkhas to continue their march to Jythuk, without further opposition; and gave them so much confidence, that they never afterwards failed to attack a post of irregulars whenever placed within their reach; and even when stockaded, they generally succeeded.

The 18-pounders, from the Black Hill, were opened

---

* Ujumba Punt was the leader of this party.

against the first stockade on the 17th of March; and on the 20th a battery was erected in a more advanced position. The effect of one day's fire of this last, was to level with the ground the whole stockade; but the Major-General, instead of following up the advantage by an immediate attack, which all the troops were eagerly expecting, came now to the conclusion that his present plan was injudicious; for that, if carried, the post could not be maintained against the force Runjoor Singh could bring up from behind it. It would thus seem, that with an European regiment and a force of at least five thousand of the Company's regular army, the Major-General yet thought it dangerous to take a step that might bring on a general action with an enemy, who had never more than two thousand five hundred men at the utmost.

This excess of caution was an unfortunate consequence of the early disasters above related; but it was a feeling that none of the officers or troops of the division participated with the General, and that, under the circumstances, was quite unwarranted. The vacillation of mind exhibited in the adoption and abandoning of these different plans, was strongly remarked upon by the Commander-in-Chief. It seemed to him that the practicability of reducing the stockades by battering them in succession, could as well have been determined upon before bringing up the guns, and wasting so much labour and ammunition; in which case, more than a month would have been saved for the prosecution of any other plan. It is painful, however, to dwell upon the sources of such disappointments.

Upon relinquishing the hope of gaining any useful end by the heavy artillery, the Major-General, on the 26th of March, came to the resolution of surrounding Runjoor by detachments, and thus reducing him by blockade and starvation. General Ochterlony, he perceived, had effected every thing by directing his efforts against the supplies of his antagonist; and there could be little doubt that the same system must be efficacious at Jythuk, though the end of March was rather late in the season to commence on such an operation. In execution of this new plan, Major Richards was sent, on the 1st of April, to seize a post on the eastern ridge, connected with Jythuk.

He marched with two battalions, the 1st of the 13th and 1st of the 15th N. I. and some irregulars. Having made a considerable circuit, to bring his detachment to a place where the ascent could be made with artillery, and without much separation of the files, he advanced cautiously to gain the top of the ridge, which was occupied by the Goorkhas in considerable force.

The enemy allowed the Major to come within forty yards before delivering his fire. The post was, however, overpowered without much loss; and Major Richards followed up his advantage along the ridge to a point called Punjab-ka-Teeba, or Punchul; where the Goorkas seemed disposed to make a more serious stand. The Major halted, to allow time for the rear companies to close up; and then attacked this post in two columns; and carrying it, proceeded immediately to make preparations to stockade it against an effort to recover it, that he expected Runjoor Singh would make with his whole force. The enemy were, however, deterred by the state of preparation they witnessed, and by their past ill-success; and left Major Richards full leisure to establish himself securely.

In the above affair the Goorkha commander, Ujumba Punt*, was taken prisoner; and of thirteen hundred men that composed his force, one hundred and seven were

---

* This was the same man, who with two hundred, or one hundred and fifty Goorkhas, defeated the irregulars under Lieutenant Young.

killed, and about two hundred and fifty wounded. The British loss was trifling, being only seven killed and twenty-nine wounded, including two officers. On the 16th of April, Captain Wilson marched to occupy a point midway between Major Richards and the headquarters of the Major-General: besides which, several other points had, in the interim, been Seized and stockaded in execution of the plan of blockade. Notwithstanding, indeed, the lateness of the period at which it was adopted, there can be but little doubt that the operation would have been effectual in reducing Jythuk, had not its fall been hastened by other means.

The glory of receiving the surrender of Jythuk was reserved for Sir David Ochterlony, whose further successes alone remain to be recorded.

We left this officer in position on the further side of the Maloun ridge, with Colonel Arnold at Rutungurh, between the enemy and Belaspoor, while Colonel Cooper was left to reduce the forts of the Ramgurh range. The first of these attacked was Ramgurh itself, which, after great exertions in dragging up the heavy artillery, was breached at last on the 16th of February. The garrison capitulated for themselves, and for Joorjooree, and were allowed to march out with the honours of war.

The two commanders, however, on joining Umur Singh at Maloun, were punished with the loss of their ears and noses—an act of savage discipline not perhaps wholly unmerited by the individuals; but considering Umur Singh's circumstances, not very judicious. Each of the forts had a garrison of one hundred men; and Joorjooree would have taken some days to reduce, even admitting that Ramgurh could have held out no longer.

It was the 10th of March before Colonel Cooper could bring a battery to bear on Taragurh, the next place he attacked. The breach was practicable the following day, and the garrison evacuated the fort in the night. Chumba, on the same ridge, was next attacked; and by the 16th of March, after a day's battering, the garrison hung out the white flag, and surrendered prisoners of war. The chiefs expressed alarm lest their families should suffer from Umur Singh's severity; to deceive him, therefore, the Colonel ordered the guns to continue firing occasionally with blank cartridges; while some of the prisoners were released, that they might endeavour to bring away the families from Maloun.

The whole of the strong forts in the rear being thus reduced and occupied, Colonel Cooper followed the main army, to take part in the last operations against Maloun. By the 14th of April all was prepared for a combined movement, the plan of which the General had for some time been maturing.

The immediate object was to effect a lodgment within the series of heights that formed Umur Singh's present position. His line stretched between the stone forts of Maloun and Soorujgurh, presenting to the view a series of connected peaks more or less abrupt, and each crowned with a stockade, excepting two, which had the names of Ryla peak and Deothul. The former was conveniently situated for operations against Soorujgurh, which it would effectually cut off from Maloun; the latter was in the very heart of the Goorkha position, and not one thousand yards from Maloun itself. It was to be expected that the whole force of the Goorkhas would oppose the occupation of Deothul, which was the main object of attack. General Ochterlony reckoned, however, that even if he failed there, the possession of Ryla would still be a great advantage: and that the movement on both points at the same time, would contribute to distract the enemy. To assist the enterprize further, a diversion was planned by other detachments, which were directed to march right upon the enemy's cantonment under the walls of Maloun.

It will be proper to explain this movement more in detail. Five columns altogether were put in motion, besides detachments for the diversion, and the following was the part assigned to each. The first from Pulta, one of the posts opposed to Soorujgurh, on the enemy's extreme right, consisted of two light companies of the 19th N. I. under Lieutenant Fleming, who, attended by a strong party of irregulars, was to make a secret night movement on Ryla, and there show a light as a signal for the movement of the other columns.

Immediately on seeing it, Captain Hamilton was to march on the same point, with his own and Lieutenant Lidlie's detachments, assembled for the purpose at Jynugur; while a grenadier battalion from head-quarters, under Major Innes, moved simultaneously in the same direction. This force was destined to support Lieutenant Fleming, and to occupy Ryla; while Major Lawrie, with the 2nd battalion of the 7th N. I. from his position at Kalee, to the right, and Lieutenant-Colonel Thompson, with the 2nd battalion of the 3d N. I. from General Ochterlony's head-quarters, were to lead each separate columns on Deothul, and two field-pieces were attached to the latter, for the defence of the position when occupied.* Two smaller detachments, one led by Captain Bowyer, and the other by Captain Showers, and consisting each of three companies, besides irregulars, were to move from opposite sides direct upon the Goorkha cantonment, in order to create the diversion, above alluded to, in aid of the occupation of Deothul.

Ryla was occupied by Lieutenant Fleming in the

---

* These two columns were to wait for daylight in the bed of the Gumrora, in order that their ascent of the heights might be simultaneous.

course of the night of the 14th; and at sight of the signal, by which it was preconcerted that notice of this event should be communicated, Captain Hamilton and Major Innes marched on the same point, and in the course of the morning established themselves, without meeting any opposition. The signal being repeated from a conspicuous station behind the General's camp, the two columns under Colonel Thompson and Major Lawrie marched immediately to the Gumrora, and waiting there till daylight, moved from opposite directions on Deothul. They just met at the last ascent, and pushed on together to seize the point, at about ten in the morning; when a contest commenced as severe as any in which our native troops have ever been engaged.

As the head of the first column approached the summit of Deothul, a picquet of not more than twenty or thirty Goorkhas charged fearlessly on the advance-guard, and occasioned a check that was near proving fatal to the success of the movement. The exertions of the officers, however, particularly of Major Lawrie, restored the men to a sense of duty, and they advanced boldly and dislodged the enemy as well from Deothul as from other posts in the immediate neighbourhood. The day was spent in desultory fighting about the position; and every exertion was made in the evening and during the night to throw up defences about Deothul, in the conviction that the struggle for the post had yet to come.

The Goorkhas had been occupied during the day in opposing and pursuing the detachments of Captains Showers and Bowyer, which had thus completely succeeded in withdrawing their attention from the main object. The former officer marched from Rutungurh, and early in the day found himself within the stockades of the enemy. He was of a peculiarly chivalrous spirit, and thinking he had instilled the same ardour and fearlessness into his men, urged them to trust only to the bayonet, and in this view he commanded them not to load.

As the column approached the cantonments, a body of Goorkhas came boldly down upon them; when Captain Showers stepped-forward to lead the projected charge: the sepoys, however, not being on ground where they could form readily, proved unequal to the trial, and the Captain was left alone to stand the shock. A personal combat ensued with the Goorkha chief and he was slain by the Captain, who happened to be an excellent swordsman. This brave officer was, however, shot dead immediately after, which completed the confusion. The detachment fled precipitately as far as Lag Village, and were pursued by the Goorkhas; this spot being, however, open, the men were rallied by Lieutenant Rutledge; and having had time to load, offered a successful opposition, and again assumed the offensive.*

Captain Bowyer, in the mean time, had marched from Kalee at daybreak, and reached the point assigned to him as a post of observation by seven in the morning; there he was attacked, and maintained himself till noon; when perceiving the entire failure of Captain Showers, and thus seeing the impossibility of converting the feint into any thing more beneficial, he commenced a retreat in the face of the enemy. The retreat was executed with field-day precision, one half of the detachment retiring to position, and the other following under cover of its fire. The Goorkhas, who had anticipated confusion, and the destruction of the column, continued engaged in a fruitless pursuit during a great part of the day, but could effect nothing beyond

---

* The author of the Sketches of the Goorkha War states that the flight and pursuit were continued till arrested by the artillery of Rutungurh, which opened on the pursuers.

occasioning a few casualties. They were thus effectually drawn away from the more important post at Deothul, which was in the mean time occupied and secured, as we have before mentioned.

The night was one of anxiety to both parties. Bhugtee Thapa, or more properly Bukhtyar Thapa, Umur Singh's best officer, saw from Soorujgurh the serious character of the operation intended; he accordingly left that place, with a chosen band, to take part in the struggle which impended. The absolute necessity of dislodging the British from Deothul, was but too apparent to Umur Singh and his council. There were, however, two complete battalions now established there, besides irregulars; and two pieces of field artillery had been brought up and placed in position, to say nothing of the works hastily prepared. The elite of the Goorkha army were in this emergency collected; and two thousand, more than could well operate at once on the broken ground of the ridge, were placed under the personal command of Bhugtee Thapa, for the attack of Deothul next morning.* Umur Singh himself also resolved to appear in the field with his youngest son, the only one with him, in order to encourage and support the attack.

Agreeably to the arrangement thus determined upon, the British position at Deothul was attacked at once on all sides where it was accessible, just at daybreak on the morning of the 16th of April. The Goorkhas came on with furious intrepidity, so much so, that several were bayoneted or cut to pieces within our works. Umur Singh stood all the while just within musquet range, with the Goorkha colours planted beside him; while Bhugtee was every where excit-

---

* This officer assured Umur Singh that he would return victorious, or not at all; and he gave notice to his two wives to prepare for their *sutee*, as he had little hope of surviving. They both sacrificed themselves on the funeral pile on which his body was burnt the next day.

ing the men to further efforts. The Goorkhas particularly aimed at gaining possession of our guns; and directed their fire with so much effect against the artillery men, that at one time three officers, Lieutenant Cartwright, Lieutenant Hutchinson of the engineers, and Lieutenant Armstrong of the pioneers, were, with one artillery man, the only persons remaining to serve them.

The British commandant at Ryla, perceiving the desperate nature of the struggle at Deothul, sent a reinforcement, with ammunition, which arrived very opportunely. After a contest of two hours' continuance without intermission, the Goorkhas being observed to slacken their efforts, it was resolved to assume the offensive, and drive them back. Major Lawrie led this charge, and Bhugtee Thapa being killed in it, the enemy was every where put to flight, and the victory decided.

There were two hundred and thirteen killed and wounded on the side of the British*; and the enemy left above five hundred men on the ground about the post of Deothul. In the course of the day they sent to request permission to seek the body of Bhugtee Thapa; and it was found, covered with wounds, close to the foot of our defences. General Ochterlony ordered it to be wrapped in shawls, and delivered to Umur Singh, in order to testify the respect his bravery had excited.

The total loss incurred in the operations of the 15th and 16th of April was, two officers, three Soobadars, four Naiks, and fifty-two Sepoys killed; and five** officers, one sergeant, and two hundred and eighty-seven men wounded.

---

* Lieut. Bagot died of his wounds, and Major Lawrie was slightly hurt: Lieutenant Gabb, light battalion, and Ensign Dalgairns, of the 3r

Taken altogether, this approached more nearly to a general action than any event that occurred in the campaign; and it was a proud triumph to the officers of the Indian army, to have achieved so complete a victory on ground which gave such great advantages to the enemy, and with numbers so nearly equal—for not one half of Sir David's army was engaged.

The dispositions for the operation exhibited wonderful skill, and the precision with which the movement of the different detachments was calculated, reflects the greatest credit on those who collected the intelligence, and furnished the materials on which the plan was combined. Lieutenant Lawtie of the engineers was the most valuable instrument of those to whose exertions the General was indebted on the occasion. This young officer had, as field-engineer, directed the operations of the late successful sieges, under Colonel Cooper; and there had not been a movement or enterprize undertaken by the division, since it took the field, that had not benefited by his professional zeal, activity, and penetration. His ardour in examining all the routes by which the Maloun position was to be approached, with a view to provide against every possible contingency or mishap, led him into exertions that produced a fever of which he died in the beginning of May *; but he had the satisfaction of first seeing the completion of the triumph he so essentially contributed to secure.

General Ochterlony, who considered nothing done while any thing remained, set himself immediately to prepare a

---

* General Ochterlony published a general order on the occasion of the death of this officer, in which he spoke in high commendation of his services and useful talents. The officers of the division, uniting in esteem of his great merit, went into mourning for him, and further subscribed for the erection of a marble monument to his memory; which now stands in the cathedral church of St. John's at Calcutta—a proud record to have been earned by so young an officer.

road for heavy artillery to Deothul; and to straiten Maloun, by closing his positions round it. The Goorkhas likewise concentrated themselves about Maloun, withdrawing their garrisons from all the positions on the further side of Deothul; and even from Soorujgurh, though a place of some strength. The evacuation of this post gave Lieutenant Murray an opportunity of showing his activity and vigilance, by intercepting and dispersing the garrison as it retired.

By the end of the first week in May, a battery was raised against Maloun; and news of the fall of Almora having reached the Goorkha camp, all the Surdars urged Umur Singh to accept terms for himself, and his son, Runjoor, at Jythuk. The old chief was, however, obstinate in refusing; and endeavoured, with much earnestness, to persuade his men, that if they did but hold out till the approaching rains the British army would be obliged to withdraw.

Seeing the pertinacity of his refusal, the Surdars began to desert with their men, until at last only about two hundred remained faithful to Umur Singh. With these he retired into the fortress of Maloun until the batteries were in readiness to open on its walls. Yielding at last to his fate, this proud chief, on the 15th of May, signed a capitulation; in which it was agreed that the Goorkha nation should retire to the east of the Kalee or Gogra; and resign to the British all the provinces from Kumaon westward. Runjoor Singh was, of course, included in these terms; and the father and son, after giving orders for the surrender of all the remaining garrisons, were safely conducted, with all who chose to accompany them, to the other side of the Kalee, as stipulated.

Many of the Goorkha soldiers took service with the British; and three battalions were, at the suggestion of Sir David Ochterlony, formed of them, and called Nuseeree battalions. A provincial corps was likewise raised for Kumaon civil duties, in order to allow a further opening for the employment of the military classes.

Thus the campaign, which in January promised nothing but disaster, finished in May by leaving in the possession of the British the whole tract of hills from the Gogra to the Sutlej. A very few words will suffice to explain the nature of the arrangements made for the occupation and management of this tract.

Kumaon was made a province of the British territory, and the Honourable Edward Gardner was appointed commissioner, with full power for the administration of its affairs. The Doon was likewise retained, and annexed ultimately, to the Seharunpoor district. The remainder of the hill country was restored to the several Rajas and chiefs from whom Umur Singh had conquered it; with exception to Subathoo, Raeengurh, Nahn, and one or two other places, which were made military posts for the Nuseeree battalions.

The principle adopted was, to place all the chiefs in precisely the same condition as they stood with respect to each other before the appearance of the Goorkhas; and to leave them each in the free enjoyment of his own, under the general protection of the British government. The following statement exhibits the names and relative importance of the principal chiefs, whom this arrangement placed in a state of protected dependence. Mr. Fraser, the Political Agent attached to the force of General Martindell, was, in the first instance, invested with the duty of introducing this system; and for that purpose, some time before the surrender of Jythuk, he undertook a journey into Gurhwal, and afterwards made a tour of the principal places in the hills, where he was instrumental in confirming the Rajas and Thakoors in the assurance of their security, and in reconciling them to the new state of things. Ultimately, Gurhwal being restored to its Raja, the superintendence of the affairs of all the western chiefs was vested in Sir David Ochterlony; on whose part a military Assistant was appointed to reside at Subathoo.

CHAPTER 5

An Uneasy Peace

In hazarding a breach with the British government, the Goorkhas had never speculated on rousing it to such exertions as they witnessed in the first campaign. Notwithstanding their early successes, therefore, they very soon repented of the rash measures by which they had brought themselves into so hopeless a contest.

Even when at the height of their prosperity, the immensity of the preparations, and the perseverance of their enemy, convinced them their cause was desperate; and they would willingly have given up every object in dispute, could they by that means have brought the war to an honourable termination.

They were prepared also for some sacrifices, if such should be required. It appears from an intercepted letter,* addressed by Umur Singh to the Raja, on the 2nd of March, 1815, that immediately on the fall of Nalapanee he was consulted as to the policy of giving up the Dehra Doon, and the hilly tract west of the Jumna, in addition to the contested lands on the Sarun and Gourukpoor frontiers.

That chief's opinion was adverse to any cession of hill territory. Though vested, therefore, with power to negotiate on this footing, if the plan had met his approval,he

---

* Appendix 1.

never indicated to General Ochterlony any disposition to treat on such a basis.*

Upon the conquest of Kumaon, the Goorkha governor of that province, Bum Sah, a man of some consideration in the state, expressed much desire to be the means of re-establishing the former relations between the two powers; and the occasion was taken of assuring the court of Katmandoo, through him, that the British government entertained a reciprocal anxiety to restore the ancient good understanding.

After the campaign had closed so triumphantly for us, the desire of peace seemed to have increased at the capital of Nepal. Most of the chiefs appeared to have become sensible that their confidence of security in the ruggedness of their mountains, was a vain illusion; and although a considerable faction still maintained their hostile disposition, all parties united in the wish to discover on what terms peace would be granted. Accordingly, in May 1815, Gooroo Gujraj Misur, the family priest of the Raja, was sent down from Katmandoo with full powers under the red seal, and with instructions to negotiate with Major Bradshaw, the British political agent in that quarter, an entire adjustment of all differences.

This overture was met by an unreserved disclosure of

---

* Some overtures were made to General Ochterlony by Umur Singh, with the view of discovering the extent of the demands of the British. When the latter, however, found that they included the cession of a considerable tract of the hill country, he proudly replied, "That from the Sutlej to the Teesta, the Goorkalees would dispute every inch of the mountains; and if driven from them, would then retire to the confines of China. This country," he added, "is not rich in men and money, like Bengal and Hindoostan; but it contains a race, of which not a man, while the soul remains in his body, will submit to become like the Rajas of the plains, with all their wealth and luxuries." Umur Singh finally refused to hold further communication with the British general, while he allowed the vakeels of the hill Rajas to remain in attendance.

the sacrifices which Lord Hastings conceived himself to be now justified in demanding. They were—1st, the perpetual cession of all the hill country taken in the campaign, *viz.* from the Kalee westward; 2ndly, a like cession of the entire Turaee, from the foot of the outer hills along the whole line of the remaining territory of the Goorkhas; 3rdly, the relinquishment by the Goorkhas of the footing they had gained in the territory of the Sikhim Raja, and the surrender to that chief of the stockaded forts of Nagree and Nagurkot; and, finally, The reception of a Resident, with the usual escort and establishment, at Katmandoo, and the customary stipulation not to receive or give service to Europeans without the special sanction of government.

Major P. Bradshaw stated to the Gooroo that he could not negotiate except on this basis; and the Gooroo declaring he had no authority to treat for any cession in the Turaee, excepting the disputed tracts, the overture was broken off, and Gujraj Misur returned to Katmandoo.

From a hope that other negotiators might be more accommodating, the Goorkha court empowered Bum Sah to make a second overture to the Honourable E. Gardner, who was now Civil Commissioner for the management of the province of Kumaon. That officer had been instructed as to the manner in which such an overture was to be received. Accordingly, the reply to Bum Sah being similar in every respect to that made to the Gooroo, the negotiation in that quarter was similarly broken off.

In the mean time, the army, which had been collected on the Sarun frontier, was cantoned to the north of the Ganges, or at Dinapoor, the cantonment of Patna, and was kept in a state of equipment to be ready to take the field immediately the favourable season should return.

The Marquess of Hastings, thinking that a second campaign might be inevitable, determined on so conducting it as to humble the proud spirit of the Goorkha chiefs; or, if that were impossible, to crush this ambitious and aspiring nation for ever. Preparation was made for penetrating with a brigade from Kumaon, where Lieutenant-Colonel J. W. Adams, a most excellent and steady officer, had succeeded Colonel Nicolls; while the latter was to operate against the Bootwul and Palpa frontier, with the army of Major-General J. S. Wood, considerably reinforced. Major-General Ochterlony was at the same time to be summoned from the north-west, to take the command of the Sarun troops, which were destined to penetrate into the valley of Nepal.

Although provision was thus made for pushing the war with vigour, the efforts of the government to re-establish peace were not relaxed; for many powerful considerations made this much the most desirable consummation at the juncture. It was with satisfaction, therefore, government learnt that the negotiation was re-opened by the Gooroo, who came again into the Turaee, in August, for the purpose. The Marquess of Hastings had, in the interim, ascertained that a main objection to the relinquishment of the Turaee was, that most of the principal officers of the Goorkha court had Jageers there. Accordingly, to reconcile them to the cession, and to show that the British government did not desire it from any avaricious motive, his Lordship authorised his negotiator to tender the amount of the estimated revenue in stipends, to be at the distribution of the court of Katmandoo. The annual assignment thus sanctioned amounted to between two and three *lacks* of rupees, and his Lordship justly considered that a permanent peace was worth this sacrifice.

The Gooroo was made acquainted with the liberal disposition of the government; but, after some consideration, he again broke off the negotiation in September; declaring that the Goorkha chiefs would never accede to a cession of the whole Turaee, which was the main source of their subsistence; the hills themselves being comparatively unproductive.

The Marquess of Hastings, having maturely weighed the matter, resolved to proceed a step further for the re-establishment of peace. It seemed evident, from what had passed, that no advantage offered in any other shape would compensate to the Goorkha government for the entire loss of the Turaee and forests under the hills. That court's repugnance to the cession was ascertained to be owing to the high estimate of the pecuniary value of the territory which was entertained by the chiefs, rather than to any feeling of pride or objection to the humiliation of the step.

The reception of a resident was the article most offensive to them on this score; but this had been insisted on as a *sine qua non*, and, finding there was no hope of procuring a change, the Goorkhas had conceded the point. The Turaee was, therefore, the only question remaining for discussion. For the last year that the British authorities had held the greater part of the tract, its management had been found very troublesome and expensive; and the climate was so noxious as to render the continuance in it of troops, and even of civil officers., impracticable for a large portion of the year.

To us, therefore, the accession of territory promised little advantage, but much trouble and difficulty in the maintenance of the rights and privileges whence the revenue was derived. The demand of the cession, it is to be observed, chiefly originated in a desire, by exclusion of the Nepalese from any interest in the lowlands, to take away the source of future contention; and, at the same time, to inflict an appropriate punishment for the encroachments, and other acts of violence and insult, which had brought on the war—the hope of profit in the tract formed no part of the motives which influenced the British government. Balancing the acquisition of the above objects, therefore, against the advantage of a restoration of peace, Lord Hastings finally determined to relax the rigour of the original terms; and a treaty was drafted, which the British negotiator was desired to present openly to the Gooroo, in case of his expected re-appearance, accompanied by a declaration that it contained the British ultimatum.

In the draft, the Turaee, from the Kalee, or western Gogra, to the Gunduk, was all that was insisted on; and of the rest, so much only as was in our actual possession. Stipends to the extent of two *lacks* of rupees were still offered to be placed at the distribution of the court, in compensation for the retained lands, and the draft contained a stipulation to this effect.

As was expected, the Raj Gooroo again sought out Major Bradshaw; and on this occasion Chundur Seekur Opadheea, who, at the close of the campaign, had been allowed to return to Katmandoo, was associated with him. The drafted treaty was shown to them, when both declared that they could not venture to accede to the terms, even as altered, without first submitting the draft to the court. They engaged, however, that a definitive answer should arrive in fifteen days, and forwarded a copy of the proposed treaty to Katmandoo for the purpose.

The term expired without their receiving any reply; and the negotiators, being unable to redeem their pledge, begged submissively that the negotiation might not be broken off, until they should themselves go to Katmandoo to ascertain the cause. The Gooroo, at the same time, offered to sign the treaty, if the portion of Turaee in the British occupation, *viz.* that lying between the Gunduk and Koosa, were substituted for the offered stipends. This was refused, and the negotiators Look their leave on the 29th of October, promising to return in twelve days, with the treaty signed.

The supreme government, on hearing of the continued reluctance of the Nepalese, called on the authorities in charge of the contiguous districts, to state their opinion as to the value of the several portions of the Turaee, and the means of obtaining a good frontier line, by the retention of part only of what had been occupied; thus preparing itself to make some further gratuitous concessions, either in *lieu* of the stipends, or in addition to them, in order the better to gratify the Goorkha chiefs, and leave them in a disposition to execute and maintain the treaty when signed.

In the mean time the Raj Gooroo Gujraj Misur came down again from Katmandoo, and signed the treaty according to the original draft. This was done at Segoulee, on the 28th of November, 1815. The supreme government, on being apprised of the event, fired the usual salutes, and ratified the treaty on the 9th of December, with due solemnity. It was determined, notwithstanding, to make the further concessions contemplated; and it was considered fortunate that the execution of the treaty without them, would yet more decidedly mark the act as a gratuitous bounty towards a fallen and suppliant foe. The conciliatory effect of the boon on the Sirdars would likewise, it was conceived, be enhanced by their not feeling themselves indebted for it to their own obstinacy either in war or negotiation.

In the confidence of its own liberal views towards the Nepalese, the British government never doubted the sincerity of the enemy. The very earnestness of their opposition in the course of the negotiation, seemed to show that the acceptance of the proffered terms was the deliberate act of the court; and though their assent was unwilling and tardy in the extreme, still this seemed to be fully accounted for by being attributed to the reluctance with which they entered into engagements they felt to be inviolable.

Adopting this view, the Governor-General reckoned that so soon as his further intentions for the benefit of the nation should be made known, the partial discontent which existed would give place to general satisfaction; and that all parties would be thankful for the restoration of peace. In this impression, the government hesitated not to suspend the preparations which had hitherto been actively making for a second campaign; and the commissariat officers, in their zeal for economy, went beyond the bounds of due discretion, and discharged a great part of the establishments which had been entertained for the transport of stores, selling also much of the grain which had been collected in the frontier depots.

Of this precipitancy there was soon reason to repent. It was a stipulation of the treaty that the ratification under the red seal should be delivered to Lieutenant-Colonel Bradshaw in fifteen days.

CHAPTER 6

A Fight for Independence

The period expired, and no ratification came; moreover, it was ascertained, in the course of the month of December, that after several very animated discussions at the court of Katmandoo, the war faction had again prevailed over that which favoured the. Gooroo, and his late negotiations. Hence a renewal of hostilities was all that could be looked for; though it was, of course, expected to be the policy of the Goorkhas to waste as much of the season of action as possible, by amusing us with fresh offers to negotiate.

In order to anticipate such an attempt, and to show the serious light in which the past conduct of the court of Katmandoo was regarded, Sir David Ochterlony was forthwith ordered into the field, and every possible exertion was made to furnish the stores and establishments requisite to give efficiency to his army. A letter was also written to the Raja of Nepal, complaining of his want of faith, and warning him of the approach of the British army. He was told, however, that the consequences might yet be averted, by sending the treaty, duly ratified, to meet the General in the Turaee.

A word or two may be required, in order to explain the motives which seemed at this time to influence the Goorkha councils. The non-ratification of the treaty of

Segoulee has not, ordinarily, been attributed to any settled plan of deceit practised on the British government; but it must be admitted, that the time of the Raj Gooroo's signing, which was just that at which the army would otherwise have taken the field, is a very suspicious circumstance. There seems reason, however, to believe that the Raj Gooroo was himself sincere, and that the disavowal of his act was the result of a divided sentiment amongst the chiefs; part of whom strenuously advocated the necessity of accepting the terms offered, while others as violently opposed the measure.

The veteran Umur Singh, and his sons, who had recently arrived at the capital, were amongst the warmest partisans of the war. Some notion of the proud spirit which actuated this chief may be formed from the intercepted letter written by him in March 1815, when he himself was closely beset on every side by the army of General Ochterlony, against which he felt he could make no head. As the document is highly characteristic, and shows the hopes which buoyed up the war faction in their determination to persevere, rather than submit to what they deemed the first step to subjection, it may not be out of place to give it at length*, though it has already been more than once before the public.

The points most dwelt upon are the following:

First—That a treaty concluded after defeat could not be trusted to, as the British, knowing the terms to be conceded through fear, would presume upon the weakness of the nation, and seek new causes of quarrel, until its absolute subjugation was effected.

Secondly—That the constitution of the Goorkha

---

* See appendices

power, which held several subordinate Rajas and nations in unwilling subjection, would afford the British numberless occasions of interference; and that they would thus by intrigue, during peace, effectually weaken and undermine the dominion established.

Thirdly—The danger of allowing a Resident to be permanently fixed at Katmandoo, is particularly dwelt upon as likely to lead to the introduction of a subsidiary force, and to prove a preliminary step to absolute subjection.

Fourthly—The advantage of manful resistance, as opposed to concession and submissiveness, is strongly urged, from the prosperity enjoyed by the Bhurtpoor Raja since his successful defence of that fortress, contrasted with the utter ruin by which Tippoo Sooltan was overtaken, after the concessions made by him to effect the peace signed by Lord Cornwallis in 1790.

The remainder of this curious letter contains an exaggerated view of the resources of the nation— first, in the courage of its troops, and the natural strength of the country; and secondly, in the support to be expected from the ill-affected allies of the British in Hindoostan, and eventually from the Chinese, to whom an immediate application for assistance in money is strongly recommended.

Assuming this letter to contain a fair statement of the sentiment of those who advocated the continuance of war, it would seem that suspicion of the ulterior views of the British was a main ingredient of their present disposition. It is certain, however, that independently of such a suspicion, the events of the past campaign in the Turaee, east of the Gogra, had filled many of the chiefs with the most presumptuous confidence in the strength of the barrier opposed by the forests and hills, which skirted their eastern territories, and that the occurrences to the west had very partially removed this feeling. From the Gogra to the Koosee, on a line of near eight hundred miles, the British armies had been wholly baffled; and though superior in force to those which achieved the conquests of the west, had not even ventured to cross the forest. Hence, the Goorkhas felt assured that they might persevere in the war with impunity, so long as they kept the passes of the first range guarded; and, under this impression, they saw no reason why they should assent to a permanent relinquishment of their independence, by receiving a Resident; or give up the ambitious hope of recovering some part of their lost territory in the hills.

CHAPTER 7

To War Again

In this state of the public feeling at Katmandoo, the treaty of Segoulee was, as we have before related, finally rejected by the chiefs; and every precaution taken to fortify and render impregnable the passes through the first range of hills. The principal route into the valley of Nepal is by the Bicheea-Koh pass, which by distinction is called the Chooreea Ghatee, or main pass over the Choorea hills. Other minor passes have occasionally the same name applied to them, or at least to that part of the route by them which leads over the same range. The grand pass, however, is, as before stated, by Bicheea Koh; and this the Goorkhas defended by three successive fortifications; the last of which was absolutely impregnable: all the other known routes were similarly defended; and in this manner the Goorkhas awaited the arrival of General Sir David Ochterlony, leaving him the passage of the forest altogether free.

The British army was already in motion to the Turaee, when towards the beginning of February, it was met by Gujraj Misur, with a formal intimation of the determination of the Nepalese to recommence the war. Sir D. Ochterlony had a force of near twenty thousand effective men, including three European regiments, His Majesty's 24th, 66th, and 87th. He divided this force into four brigades: giving Colonel Kelly, of the 24th, one; Lieutenant-Colonel Nicol, of the 66th, another; Lieutenant-Colonel Miller, of the 87th, a third; while the fourth was commanded by Colonel Dick, who has before been mentioned.

Colonel Kelly, with his brigade and regiment, were detached to the right by Bhugwanpoor, with orders to penetrate, if possible, by Hureehurpoor; Lieutenant-Colonel Nicol was similarly directed on Ramnugur, to the left; while General Ochterlony, with the other two brigades, moved straight through the forest, by Simlabassa, to the foot of the Bicheea Koh pass.

On the 10th of February, 1816, the General established himself at a kind of *caravanseray* at the outlet of the pass, and at a short distance from the enemy's first stockade. The *seray* was quickly converted into a depot; and the opposite works having been reconnoitered, and found unassailable, information was sought with earnestness as to the possibility of turning the pass by some route unknown to the enemy.

After four days thus spent, without interruption of any kind from the Goorkha army, a route was discovered by Captain Pickersgill, of the Quartermaster-General's department; and on the 14th, at nine at night, Colonel Miller's brigade was led by the General in person through a deep and narrow ravine, called Baleekola, which brought the detachment to a water-course, leading to a steep acclivity, by which the first formidable barrier of hills was to be scaled. The march was continued during the whole night, and by seven in the morning, the Choorea heights, to the west of the enemy's positions, were occupied without resistance. In the course of the 15th, the brigade advanced about five miles to the Chukree Mukree *nulla*, and there bivouacked for four days, waiting the arrival of its supplies and tents, for no laden animal had been able to accompany the troops.

For the first two days the men suffered the greatest privations, being for the most part without food. Their hardships were participated, in a great measure, by the General himself, who had no baggage, and slept under cover of a hut, hastily constructed for him by the men of the 87th, of boughs cut from the green trees. All this, however, was submitted to with cheerfulness by both men and officers, in the conviction that the object of the movement was gained. On the morning following that of the General's march, Colonel Dick moved up close to the enemy's outer stockade; and, in the course of the following day, found the triple fortification evacuated by the Goorkhas, in consequence of the success of the operation for turning the position.

By the 20th of February, the roads were prepared for a further advance; and the two brigades met again at Etounda, on the banks of the Raptee, which here runs in a valley remarkably picturesque and beautiful. After a halt to establish a second depot, the Major-General marched again on the 27th, moving up the valley to Mukwanpoor, under which place he encamped in the evening, at a village called Chougurha Mundee.

Mukwanpoor is situated on a low ridge, which lay to the north of the encampment, stretching from west to east. The town and fort were to the east opposed to our right, and on the other extremity was a village named Seekhur Kutree, which was also occupied by the enemy on the General's first appearance under the position.

For some unknown reason, the Goorkhas withdrew their men from Seekhur Kutree next morning, which being observed by the British General, he immediately detached four companies and forty Europeans to seize the point. Captain Pickersgill accompanied them, and was proceeding to occupy some other points along the ridge, when he perceived a large force of the enemy ascending the northern side of the hill, so as to cut him off from Seekhur Kutree, which he had just left. He made good his retreat down the southern declivity into camp, while the Goorkhas advanced against the posts which had been occupied. They had recovered all but the village itself, and the men there had lost their commanding officer, Lieutenant Tirrell,* and were beginning to feel the want of ammunition, when the 25th N. I. which General Ochterlony had kept under arms prepared for any exigency, came opportunely to their relief, accompanied by the flank companies of the 87th.

The post was now secured, and dispositions made to maintain it; but the Goorkhas, unwilling to relinquish the advantage, poured a force of two thousand men from the stockade near Mukwanpoor, and showed a determination to recover the village at all hazards. Sir David Ochterlony, seeing that the contest was becoming every instant more serious, detached the 2nd battalion of the 12th N. I. with four more companies of the 87th, under the command of Colonel Miller, to support the troops at Seekhur Kutree; and turning out his line, he further ordered the artillery to play on the different bodies of the enemy as they passed along the ridge to the attack.

The Goorkhas seeing this, opened also their guns at Mukwanpoor, turning them at first against the advancing parties, and subsequently on the camp and line where Sir David and his staff were a conspicuous object.** In the

---

* This officer was Adjutant of the 1st battalion of the 20th, or Marine Regiment, but was at the time doing duty with the 2nd battalion of the 25th, having left his staff situation to seek distinction in the active service of this campaign. He had only joined by Dak a day or two before. The post was maintained after the fall of Lieutenant Tirrell, by Lieutenant Kerr and Ensign Impey, who were publicly thanked in general orders for the service.
** A menial servant of the General's, who carried his pen and ink, was killed by this fire; but, in other respects, it did remarkably little execution.

mean time, the junction of the reinforcement enabled the force at Seekhur Kutree to advance on the enemy; and the Europeans leading, a charge was made, which drove the Goorkhas beyond a hollow separating this part of the ridge from Mukwanpoor. Detached parties of the enemy, however, still cowered down in the *jungul* on the ridge, and kept up a very destructive, though desultory fire on our posts; they brought also some guns to the opposite side of the hollow, and thus continued to annoy us during the whole day.*

Towards the afternoon, Sir David Ochterlony despatched to Colonel Miller a fresh battalion, the 2nd of the 8th N. I., to enable him to finish the action, if possible, before sunset. The battalion, upon its arrival, was conducted by Major Nation across the hollow; and advancing with charged bayonets, captured the nearest of the enemy's guns: after which, the Goorkhas retired within their fort and stockades, leaving their dead and wounded at our mercy.

The Goorkhas were, in this action, led by Shumsheer Rana, the chief who commanded the attack on Captain Sibley's post at Pursa in the previous campaign. Their

---

* In the duty of this day many officers found great advantage in the use of their double-barrelled fowling-pieces, with the skill acquired by practice in the sports of the field. The officer who commanded the light company of the 25th N. I. was particularly distinguished for the certainty with which he anticipated the aim of the Goorkha light troops, who ordinarily lay secure under a rock, presenting nothing except just at the moment of firing. Ensign Shipp, of his Majesty's 87th, was noticed for a personal encounter with a Goorkha chief, in the face of both armies. He was a capital swordsman, but his weapon broke early in the conflict, whereupon, he threw it away, and trusting to his activity, closed with the Goorkha, and wrenching his sword from him, laid him lifeless with a back-handed stroke.—Feats of this kind are not the proper duty of officers, but when they occur are very encouraging to the troops; for the union of personal prowess with gallantry and success will always command admiration.

whole force was engaged in the course of the day, and the defeat was signal; their loss in killed and wounded having, by their own acknowledgment, exceeded eight hundred men. Of the British, forty-five were killed, including eleven men of the 87th; and one hundred and seventy-five wounded, including nineteen Europeans, and Lieutenant and Adjutant P. Young, of the 2nd battalion the 12th N. I.; Lieutenant Tirrell was the only officer killed.

Colonel Nicol, with his brigade, joined the Major-General on the day after the action; having successfully penetrated into the valley of the Raptee, by a pass to the north of Ramnugur, and having marched thence up the valley without meeting any opposition. The Colonel left a strong detachment of two battalions in position at Ekoor, under Major Lumley, to maintain the communication by this route, and keep the valley free of the enemy.

In the mean time Colonel Kelly, who had orders to penetrate by Hureehurpoor, succeeded likewise in finding a route by which he entered the hills without opposition, and penetrated to that fortress. His march was, however, much impeded by the difficulties of the ground; and it was the 27th of February before he reached Rutunpoor, a village on the left bank of the Bagmutee, a few miles to the south of the fort. He immediately made from hence a strong reconnoisance; and finding the post to be unassailable from the south, he resolved on crossing the Bagmutee and advancing to Joorjoor, a village to the west of Hureehurpoor, whence the approach seemed more easy.

This movement was effected on the 29th of February. The principal stockade of the enemy was about one thousand yards to the west of Hureehurpoor, crowning the ridge in a semicircular form, and commanding the valley of the Bagmutee. On the Colonel's first arrival at Joorjoor, he observed an eminence at about eight hundred yards distance from this stockade, which the enemy had left unoccupied. He, accordingly, next morning, before daybreak, detached his light companies, under Captain (Brevet-Major) Hughes, of his Majesty's 24th, supported by seven battalion-companies, under Lieutenant-Colonel O'Holloran, to seize the point.

This detachment ascended, and quickly established itself, driving off a picquet of the enemy it found there; no sooner, however, was it well in position, than the whole force of the Goorkhas came on to the attack; and Colonel O'Holloran had to sustain an unequal fight from six in the morning until half-past eleven, exposed on every side to the fire of the enemy. At length a strong reinforcement arrived, with two 6-pounders, and two howitzers on elephants. The enemy was then driven back with considerable loss, and the attempt on the position was not repeated*.

The Goorkhas, indeed, although their first attack was vigorous and obstinate, did not evince, on this occasion, quite so much bravery as was expected from the reputation of their commander; who was no other than Runjoor Singh, the defender of Jythuk. He had with him also a choice band of his associates in that defence, whom he had distinguished by crescents on their turbans, and by the pompous title of 'Band of the Moon'. Runjoor was himself one of the first to leave the field; and his conduct in the action, and in subsequently abandoning his post, tarnished his bright name, and brought him into permanent disgrace at the court of Katmandoo. The fort of Hureehurpoor was evacuated in the night after this af-

---

* The British loss consisted of four Europeans and four Natives, killed; five officers—Captain Lindsay, artillery; Captain (Brevet-Major) Hughes, Captain Smith, and Lieutenant O'Leary, of his Majesty's 24th; Lieutenant De Voeux, Chumparun Light Infantry; twenty-three Europeans, and twenty-five Natives, wounded.

fair; and Colonel Kelly, having converted it into a depot, was preparing for a further advance, when he received the General's orders to retrace his steps.

The news of the first defeat at Mukwanpoor, spread consternation at Katmandoo; and without waiting for intelligence of the event at Hureehurpoor, the court immediately resolved on an attempt to deprecate further vengeance by unqualified submission. The red seal was affixed in haste to the treaty of Segoulee; and an envoy sent to the camp of General Ochterlony, to notify that it was ready for delivery. The messenger brought a letter from Bukhtawur Singh, the Goorkha commander, requesting permission to send the instrument by Chundur Seekur Opadheea, who was stated to have come to Mukwanpoor for the purpose. The General returned for answer, that the Goorkhas must not expect the same terms now, as before the recommencement of hostilities; but that he had no objection to receive the Opadheea if he came with full powers. At the same time the approaches were pushed on to within five hundred yards of Mukwanpoor, and a battery was made ready against the place.

Chundur Seekur made his appearance in camp on the 3rd of March, and earnestly entreated the General to accept the ratified treaty. Sir David had been vested with full powers to use his own discretion, in the acceptance of the former terms, or in advancing further demands, according as circumstances and the state of the season might prompt; but he was not to conclude a treaty until the enemy were sufficiently humbled to make it safe to rely on their sincerity.

This period seemed to Sir David to have now arrived; and in order to put their humility to the test, it was explained to Chundur Seekur, that the letter of the treaty would give to the British all the territory in their occupation, and would now, therefore, include the valley of the Raptee, as well as Hetounda and Hureehurpoor. At the same time the Opadheea was assured that he must no longer expect any concession beyond the letter, and he was called upon to give a specific note in writing, declaratory of his being influenced by no such hopes, and further to engage that the Raja should specifically confirm the declaration in a letter to the Governor-General.

To all this the Goorkha negotiator readily assented; and he agreed, moreover, to present the ratified treaty on his knees at the General's *durbar*, in the presence of all the Vakeels in camp.

This solemnity having passed, the General concluded the treaty, and despatched Lieutenant Boileau of his staff to act as Resident at Katmandoo, until the Governor-General should nominate a proper officer. He prepared, also, for his own return; but did not finally leave the hills until he received the orders for the surrender of the forts of Nagree and Nagurkot to the Raja of Sikhim, and had ascertained that they would be duly executed.

Lord Hastings was much pleased with the result to which Major-General Ochterlony had thus brought the campaign in so short a space of time; more particularly so, because the late period at which the operations had unavoidably been undertaken, after the interruption to the preparations, which occurred in November and December, had made him apprehensive of the arrival of the unhealthy season before there would be time effectually to humble the enemy. Sir David himself, too, had discovered that the capture of Mukwanpoor would be the limit of what could be effected this campaign; for he found it would not be safe to keep the troops in that valley after the middle of March; this, therefore, was not the least powerful of the motives which influenced him in granting the terms.

The articles of the treaty were all punctually executed, according to agreement.* The supreme government
thought, notwithstanding what had passed, that it would be
a politic act of conciliation to give up such of the Turaee as
might not be required to form a straight and even frontier,
in lieu of the pensions stipulated in the treaty. The Marquess of Hastings, therefore, after every article had been
executed, gave notice to the Raja of his intention to send
the Honourable E. Gardner to Katmandoo, as Resident,
and to empower him to conclude a new arrangement on
that basis. This was subsequently effected, after a boundary
had been surveyed and marked with pillars of masonry, to
prevent the possibility of any future disputes between the
Nepalese officers and our Zemindars.

The part of the Turaee which skirted the Oudh dominions was, however, retained, and with Khyreegurh,
a *perguna* of Rohilkhund, lying on the Oudh side of the
Gogra, was made over to the Nuwab Vizeer, in extinc-
tion of the second loan of a *crore* of rupees obtained from
him during the war.

With the Sikhimputee Raja a treaty was concluded by
Major Latter, at Titaleea, on the 10th of February, 1817,**
in which, amongst other articles, there is one guaranteeing
the possessions of the Raja to himself and his family—a
small stripe of the Turaee also, lying between the Michhee
and the Teesta, (part of what was retained under the final
arrangements concluded with Nepal), was ceded to this
Raja for a line of communication.

The policy of this guarantee cannot be doubted. Its effect has been to shut out the Nepalese from any ambitious
views of aggrandizement to the east, and to circumscribe
their territory on three sides by the British power, while

---

* Appendix

** Appendix

on the fourth, the stupendous range of the Heemalaya, and the Chinese frontier, present an effectual barrier. Thus, while the British and Chinese empires continue in their present strength, the hope of extending their dominion must be extinguished, and the military spirit, which was fostered by the series of victories gained over the surrounding Rajas, must die away for want of employment.

CHAPTER 8

No Help from the Chinese

It only now remains to state the nature of the relations subsisting between the government of Nepal, and the Celestial Empire, and the result of the application made to Pekin for assistance, during the campaign of 1814-15.

In the first government of Lord Cornwallis, the Goorkhas having invaded Tibet, and plundered the palace of the Teeshoo Lama, at Jigurchee or Digurchee, a Chinese army was sent to punish them. The Goorkhas retired before it, but contrived to maintain themselves for some time without much loss.

This produced an overture from the Chinese commander, that the British should co-operate in a simultaneous attack on Nepal. The proposition was not favourably received; and the Chinese, having changed their General, gained an important victory in the Tingree desert, and thus succeeded at last in reducing the Goorkhas to submission. From that time Nepal has been considered by the Chinese as a tributary country; and though nothing is demanded beyond some nominal offerings, still a legation proceeds every three years from Katmandoo, to renew the assurances of allegiance and good faith.

On the war breaking out with the British, the Nepalese represented to the court of Pekin that the difference had arisen in consequence of our having demanded the passes through the Heemachul, which they, as faithful allies, had refused to give. The Chinese attached no credit to the representation, until they received, through their own officers at Lassa, a long manifesto; which the Supreme Government, knowing the relations which existed between Katmandoo and the Celestial Empire, thought it expedient to forward in explanation of the real cause of war.

The Chinese now argued that there might probably be some truth in what the Goorkhas had represented of our ambitious views, as so much pains was taken to disavow, or, as they conceived, to disguise them. Accordingly, it was determined by the Court of Pekin that a force should immediately be directed to the quarter menaced; and that one of the most confidential ministers, and a military man, should proceed to ascertain the state of things in Nepal.

So slow were the Chinese in executing their determination, that the war was actually over before their army was heard of at Katmandoo. In September 1816, however, the Governor-general received, through the Sikhim Raja, a letter, written in scarcely intelligible Persian, from a person styling himself Shee Cheeoon Chang, Vizier, or Prime Minister, with whom were associated the chief authority of Lassa, and another principal officer of the frontier. The object of the letter was, to ask distinctly what were the views of the British government in that direction,* and to state how they had been misrepresented. In the course of the same month, the Goorkhas, having heard that a Chinese force had arrived at Digurchee, or Jigurchee, in August, applied directly to the Resident to know whether, in case the Chinese demanded any fur-

---

* The Bengal government had furnished the Company's officers at Canton with a full explanation of all that passed; but the Chinese cautiously avoided any allusion to the Nepal war in their official communications with the select committee there.

ther submission beyond what had already been acceded to, they might depend on the co-operation of the British in resisting them.

In this state of things, the Supreme Government forbad any assurance of support being given to the Nepalese, lest it should encourage them in seeking cause of quarrel with the Chinese. The Governor-general also communicated a statement of all that had occurred, in reply to the letter which had been received through the Sikhim Raja. With this answer the Chinese authorities professed themselves satisfied, in so far as the British were concerned: they demanded, however, that some confidential agents from Nepal should wait upon them; and the following account of what passed at the interview, was obtained afterwards from a Cashmeerian of the suite.

The first visit was one of pure ceremony; but the Goorkha Vakeels, Dilbunjun Pande and Colonel Runbeer Singh Thapa, waited again on Cheeoon Chang on the following day, when his Excellency commenced by asking, "What had become of the Pandes and Bishnawuths?" (leaders of the expedition into Tibet before alluded to;) and he added, "Who are these Thapas that I never before heard of? You Goorkhas are a mischievous race, and have caused the ruin of many Rajas. Digurchee, too, you plundered without cause or provocation; and now you have thought to act the Digurchee scene with the English, and so murdered their police-officer, after settling the question by negotiation. You have been punished justly—you wrote us of war, and have since written of peace; yet still ask our aid.—What kind of peace is this?"

The Nepalese urged that if not inclined to give assistance to recover what had been lost, the Chinese authorities would, at least, lend their good offices to procure the removal of the Residency from Katmandoo.

Cheeoon Chang replied, "You wrote that it was to establish a factory that the English had come; why should I remove merchants?"

Dilbunjun, one of the Vakeels, on this said, "They were not merchants, but soldiers and officers that they desired to be rid of."

Cheeoon Chang replied, "The English have written that their object is to cement peace; I and it appears you have agreed to receive the Resident. You wrote us that the English had demanded the passes into Koten China; but we know this is false—if they desired to come to China, it would not be by that route." Turning to Colonel Runbeer, the other Vakeel, Cheeoon Chang continued in a tone of irony, "You Goorkhas think the hills have no soldiers but yourselves: how many of you may there be? About two *lakh*, I suppose!—and what is your revenue?"

Runbeer replied, "That his Excellency was right in the number of fighting men; and that the revenue of the hill country was very small, not exceeding five *lakh* of rupees."

"Truly," said Cheeoon Chang, "you are a mighty nation!" and with this he dismissed the Vakeels.

The Chinese were so fully satisfied with the intelligence procured on this occasion, that they immediately withdrew their troops from Digurchee and Lassa. They betrayed, however, a little jealousy at the establishment of a Resident at Katmandoo; and, in reply to the letter of the Governor-General, after stating that they were perfectly satisfied, the Vizier introduced a hint that they should be still better pleased were he withdrawn. It was couched in the following terms.

"You mention that you have stationed a Vakeel in Nepal. This is a matter of no consequence; but as the Raja, from his youth and inexperience, and from the novelty of

126

the thing, has imbibed some suspicions, if you would, out of kindness towards us, and in consideration of the ties of friendship, withdraw your Vakeel from thence, it would be better, and we should feel very much obliged to you."

These minute details are, perhaps, too puerile to be recorded at such length; but as so little is known of the conduct pursued by the Chinese In their relations with other Asiatic powers, at the same time that there is an interest about every thing that brings us politically into contact with them, it is hoped that this full account of their proceedings at Digurchee will not prove unamusing or out of place.

To the above statement of occurrences after the treaty, it only remains to add, that the young Raja of Nepal died, on the 20th of November 1816, of the small-pox; and was succeeded by an infant son named Raj Indur Bikrum Sah. This event contributed to fix more firmly the authority of the party of General Bheem Sein, by giving him another lease of uncontrolled dominion, pending a second long minority.

Appendices

Appendix 1

Translation of a copy of the written Opinions of the Principal Goorkha Chiefs, on the Question of Peace or War with the British Government

Question submitted by the Raja of Nepal

Disputes exist between me and the English. The Governor-General has written to me that he has given orders to the Judge and Collector to establish their authority, (in the disputed lands on the Gourukpoor frontier,) and that he shall not think it necessary to repeat his intimation on that subject. How then is my Raj to exist? In my judgment, an appeal should be made to arms. Do you deliberate, and give me a decided and united opinion.

Reply of General Bheem Sein Thapa

Through the influence of your good fortune, and that of your ancestors, no one has yet been able to cope with the state of Nepal. The Chinese once made war upon us, but were reduced to seek peace. How then will the English be able to penetrate into the hills? Under your auspices, we shall by our own exertions be able to oppose to them a force of fifty-two *lakhs* of men, with which we will expel them. The small fort of Bhurtpoor was the work of man, yet the English, being worsted before it, desisted from the attempt to conquer it; our hills and fastnesses are formed by the hand of God, and are impregnable. I therefore recommend the prosecution of hostilities. We can make peace afterwards on such terms as may suit our convenience.

Reply of Kajee Rundoj Singh Thapa

What General Bheem Sein has stated is good. Alexander overthrew empires, but failed to establish his authority in our mountains. There is, however, one source of apprehension. The Hill Rajas have been expelled from their dominions. They will disclose the secrets of the hills, and will assuredly conduct the English into those regions. When the Rajas shall unite and co-operate with the English, the latter will acquire confidence, and force their way into the country. I therefore recommend a temporizing policy for a time, or even to concede a portion of what is now actually in their possession, as preferable to war. By such a course, the machinations and intrigues of our enemies will best be defeated. I have thus stated what has occurred to my mind.

Reply of Raj Gooroo Rungnat Pundit

I conceive that the will of the Sovereign is paramount to all other considerations, but having been asked my opinion, I proceed to deliver it, leaving the Sovereign to adopt it or otherwise at his pleasure. Hitherto we have contrived to effect our purpose one way or another, but for the future, it seems to me that without an adjustment of the boundary dispute to their satisfaction, the English will not recede. As yet we have received no injury (calling for an appeal to arms); I propose, therefore, that of the territory of the Nuwab Vizeer, which has come into the possession of this state, (meaning of the usurpations on the Gourukpoor frontier,) half should be relinquished as the price of peace. If the English resolve on hostilities, we cannot maintain ourselves in those possessions, for we cannot cope with them in the plains or Turaee, though in the hills we have nothing to fear. I have thus stated my opinion, but am at the same time ready to yield to the better judgment of others.

Reply of Kajee Dilbunjun Pande (or Panre)

The Gooroo has made himself personally acquainted with the designs and proceedings of the English, and conceives them to be decidedly inimical. It is well. But are we inferior to the English, that we should yield to them? They cannot invade our territory: if they attempt it, they must be repulsed; for should they once succeed in penetrating, all the concerns of this Raj will be thrown into confusion. If their efforts are directed against the Turaee of this state, and they excite disturbances there, can we not retaliate? And how will they be able to protect their own territories?

Reply of Chountra Bum Sak—of Kajee Umur Singh Thapa—and of Hustodeel

We have enough to do to manage the territory we possess. But if circumstances drive us into war with the English, by the influence of the auspicious fortune of this Raj, we should fight and conquer. The present time however is not favourable. The English, seeing their opportunity, have put themselves into an attitude of offence, and the conflict, if war be now undertaken, will be desperate. They will not rest satisfied without establishing their own power and authority, and will unite with the Hill Rajas, whom we have dispossessed. We have hitherto but hunted deer; if we engage in this war, we must prepare to fight tigers. If the Raja would listen to our advice, we would recommend the relinquishment, for the present, of all lands recently occupied, so as to avoid a rupture. For if matters be pushed to extremity with the English, the whole concerns of the state will be thrown into confusion. Matters in this quarter (i. e. in the western hills, of which these three chiefs were governors) are already in a distracted condition, and other parts of the Goorkha territory will similarly become the scene of disorder. The advocate of war, he who proposes to fight and conquer the English (alluding to Bheem Sein,) has been bred up at court, and is a stranger to the toil and hardships of a military life. Even now that he proposes war, his place is about your person. By the influence of the auspicious fortune of this Raj success would crown our efforts in the event of a rupture: but our life has been passed in traversing forests, with hatchets in our hands to collect wood and leaves, and still we pursue the same occupation. War we know to be an arduous undertaking; it is so for veteran troops, and for raw recruits must be much more so. There is an old saying, that they best transact their master's business who exercise the greatest prudence and circumspection.

Translation of Instructions sent by the Raja of Nepal to General Umur Singh Thapa, governor of Palpa, on the Gourukpoor frontier

I send you a copy of the opinions of all the principal chiefs. They differ widely from one another; but the result is a determination for war. Purchase, therefore, and lay up in store, all the grain you can procure, and send an account of the treasure and gunpowder at your command. Establish a chain of posts from Sooleana to the Gunduk river, and entertain all the recruits you can. Let the property of all persons between the ages of twelve and forty, who may refuse to join in the war, be confiscated, and allow every man a *seer* of rice for subsistence while he may serve. I have issued orders for calling out the population here, and for establishing a chain of posts along the frontier. You must strengthen the forts of Nonakoh. Five hundred Telingas (regular sepoys) will be despatched to reinforce the troops under your command.

Send daily reports of what passes in your quarter, and prepare for active hostilities.

Dated, *Chyt*, 1871, *Sunbut*,

corresponding with 2nd April, 1814.

Appendix 2

From Umur Singh and his sons, Ram Das, and Urjun Thapas, to the Raja of Nepal, dated Raj-gurh, 2nd March, 1815.

A copy of your letter of the 23rd December, addressed to Runjoor Singh, under the Red Seal, was sent by the latter to me, who have received it with every token of respect. It was to the following purport:

"The capture of Nalapanee by the enemy has been communicated to me from Gurhwal and Kumaon, as also the intelligence of his having marched to Nahn: having assembled his force, he now occupies the whole country from Barapursa to Subturee and Muhotree. My army is also secretly posted in various places in the *junguls* of the mountains. An army under a general has arrived in Gourukpoor, for Palpa, and another detachment has reached the borders of Beejypoor. I have further heard that a general-officer has set off from Calcutta, to give us further trouble. For the sake of a few trifling objects, some intermediate agents have destroyed the mutual harmony, and war is waging far and wide. All this you know. You ought to send an embassy to conciliate the English, otherwise the cause is lost. The enemy, after making immense preparations, have begun the war, and unless great concessions are made, they will not listen to terms. To restore the relations of amity by concession is good and proper; for this purpose it is fit, in the first place, to cede to the enemy the departments of Bootwul, Palpa, and Sheeoraj, and the disputed tracts already settled by the commissioners towards Barah.* If this be insufficient to re-establish harmony, we ought to abandon the whole of the Turaee, the Doon, and the low lands; and if the English are still dissatisfied on account of not obtaining possession of a portion of the mountains, you are herewith authorized to give up, with the Doon, the country as far as the Sutlej. Do whatever may be practicable to restore the relations of peace and amity, and be assured of my approbation and assent. If these means be unsuccessful, it will be very difficult to preserve the integrity of my dominions from Kunka Teestta to the Sutlej. If the enemy once obtain a footing in the centre of our territory, both extremities will be thrown into disorder. If you can retire with your army and military stores to pursue any other; plan of operations that may afterwards appear eligible, it will be advisable. On this account, you ought immediately to effect a junction with all the other officers on the western service, and retire to any part of our territory which, as far as Nepal, you may think yourself capable of retaining. These are your orders."

In the first place, after the immense preparations of the enemy, he will not be satisfied with all these concessions, or if he should accept of our terms, he would serve us as he did Tippoo; from whom he first accepted of an indemnification of six *crores* of rupees in money and territory, and afterwards wrested from him his whole country. If we were to cede to him so much country, he would seek some fresh occasion of quarrel, and at a future opportunity, would wrest from us

---

* Meaning the twenty-two villages on the Sarun frontier.

other provinces. Having lost so much territory, we should be unable to maintain our army on its present footing, and our military fame being once reduced, what means should we have left to defend our eastern possessions? While we retain Bisahur, Gurhwal is secure: if the former be abandoned, the Bhooteas of Ruwain will certainly betray us. The English having thus acquired the Doon and Ruwain, it will be impossible for us to maintain Gurhwal; and being deprived of the latter, Kumaon and Dotee will be also lost to us. After the seizure of these provinces, Achain, Joomlee, and Dooloo, will be wrested from us in succession. You say, that "a proclamation has been issued to the inhabitants of the eastern *kurats*"; if they have joined the enemy, the other *kurats* will do so likewise, and then the country, Dood Koosee, on the east, to Bheeree, on the west, cannot be long retained. Having lost your dominions, what is to become of your great military establishments?

When our power is once reduced, we shall have another Knox's mission, under pretence of concluding a treaty of alliance and friendship, and founding commercial establishments. If we decline receiving their mission, they will insist; and if we are unable to oppose force, and desire them to come unaccompanied with troops, they will not comply. They will begin by introducing a company; a battalion will soon after follow, and at length an army will be assembled for the subjection of Nepal. You think that if, for the present, the low lands, the Doon, and the country to the Sutlej, were ceded to them, they would cease to entertain designs upon the other provinces of Nepal: do not trust them! They who counselled you to receive the mission of Knox,* and permit the establishment of a commercial factory, will usurp the

---

* Meaning apparently that the British would restore the fallen faction of the Pandes, and by their means govern Nepal.

government of Nepal. With regard to the concessions now proposed, if you had, in the first instance, decided upon a pacific line of conduct, and agreed to restore the departments of Bootwuland Sheeoraj, as adjusted by the commissioners, the present contest might have been avoided. But you could not suppress your desire to retain these places, and, by murdering their revenue officer, excited their indignation, and kindled a war for trifles.

At Jythuk we have obtained a victory over the enemy. If I succeed against General Ochterlony, and Runjoor Singh, with Juspao Thapa and his officers, prevail at Jythuk, Runjeet Singh will rise against the enemy. In conjunction with the Seiks, my army will make a descent into the plains; and our forces, crossing the Jumna from two different quarters, will recover possession of the Doon. When we reach Hurdwar, the Nuwab of Lukhnow may be expected to take a part in the cause; and, on his accession to the general coalition we may consider ourselves secure as far as Khunka. Relying on your fortune, I trust that Bulbhudur Koonwur, and Rewunt Kajee, will soon be able to reinforce the garrison of Jythuk; and I hope, ere long, to send Punt Kajee with eight companies, when the force there will be very strong. The troops sent by you are arriving every day; and when they all come up, I hope we shall succeed both here and at Jythuk.

Formerly, when the English endeavoured to penetrate to Sundowlee, they continued for two years* in possession of Bareh Pursa, and Muhotree; but, when you conquered Nepal, they were either destroyed by your force, or fell victims to the climate, with the exception of a few only, who abandoned the place. Orders should now be given

---

* Alluding to the expedition under Major Kinloch, when the Turaee was occupied for two years; an event that Umur Singh was old enough to have witnessed.

to all your officers to defend Choudundee, and Choudena in Bejypoor, and the two *kurats*, and the ridge of Mahabharut. Suffer the enemy to retain the low lands for a couple of years: measures can afterwards be taken to expel them. Lands transferred under a written agreement cannot again be resumed; but if they have been taken by force, force may be employed to recover them. Fear nothing, even though the Seiks should not join us. Should you succeed now in bringing our differences to an *amicable* termination by the cession of territory, the enemy, in the course of a few years, would be in possession of Nepal, as he took possession of the country of Tippoo. The present, therefore, is not the time for treaty and conciliation. These expedients should have been tried before the murder of the revenue officer (in Gourukpoor), or must be postponed till victory shall crown our efforts. If they will then accede to the terms which I shall propose, it is well; if not, with the favour of God, and your fortune and bounty, it shall be my business to preserve the integrity of my country from Khunka to the Sutlej. Let me intreat you, therefore, never to make peace.

Formerly, when some individuals urged the adoption of a treaty of peace and commerce, I refused my assent to that measure; I will not now suffer the honour of my prince to be sullied by concession and submission. If you are determined on this step, bestow the humiliating office on him who first advised it. But for me, call me to your presence; I am old, and only desire once more to kiss your feet. I can recollect the time when the Goorkha army did not exceed twelve thousand men. Through the favour of Heaven, and by the valour of your forefathers, your territory was extended to the confines of Khunka, on the east. Under the auspices of your father, we subjugated Kumaon; and, through your fortune, we have pushed our conquests to the Sutlej. Four generations have been employed in the acquisition of all this dignity and dominion. At Nalapanee, Bulbhudur defeated three or four thousand of the enemy. At Jythuk, Runjoor Singh, with his officers, overthrew two battalions. In this place, I am surrounded, and daily fighting with the enemy, and look forward with confidence to victory. All the inhabitants and chiefs of the country have joined the enemy. I must gain two or three victories before I can accomplish the object I have in view, of attaching Runjeet Singh to our cause. On his accession, and after the advance of the Seiks and Goorkhas towards the Jumna, the chiefs of the Dukhun may be expected to join the coalition, as also the Nuwab of Lukhnow, and the Salik-Ramee-Leech*. Then will be the time for us to drive out the enemy, and recover possession of the low countries of Palpa, as far as Bejypoor. If we succeed in regaining these, we can attempt further conquest in the plains.

There has been no fighting in your quarter yet; the Choudundee and Choudena of Beejypoor, as far as the ridge of Muhabharut and Sooleeana, should be well defended. Countries acquired in four generations, under the administration of the Thapas, should not be abandoned for the purpose of bringing matters to an amicable adjustment, without deep and serious reflection. If we are victorious in the war, we can easily adjust our differences; and if we are defeated, death is preferable to a reconciliation on humiliating terms. When the Chinese army invaded Nepal, we implored the mercy of Heaven by offerings to the Brahmins, and the performance of religious ceremonies; and, through the favour of one and intercession of the other, we succeeded in repulsing the enemy.

---

* It is not known who Umur Singh means by the Salik-Kamee-Leech; and some other of his names of places and persons differ from any in common use.

Ever since you confiscated the Jageers of the Brahmins, thousands have been in distress and poverty. Promises were given that they should be restored at the capture of Kangrah; and orders to this effect, under the red seal, were addressed to me, and Nyn Singh Thapa. We failed, however, in that object, and now there is universal discontent. You ought, therefore, to assemble all the Brahmins, and promise to restore to them their lands and property, in the event of your conquering and expelling the English. By these means, many thousand worthy Brahmins will put up their prayers for your prosperity, and the enemy will be driven forth. By the practice of charity, the territory acquired in four generations may be preserved, and through the favour of God, our power and dominion may be still further extended. By the extension of territory, our military establishment may be maintained on its present footing, and even increased: the numerous countries which you propose to cede to the enemy, yielded a revenue equal to the maintenance of an army of four thousand men, and Kangrah might have been captured. By the cession of these provinces, the reputation and splendour of your court will no longer remain. By the capture of Kangrah your name would have been rendered formidable; and though that has not happened, a powerful impression has, nevertheless, been made on the people of the plains by the extension of your conquests to the Sutlej.

To effect a reconciliation, by the cession of the country to the west of the Jumna, would give rise to the idea that the Goorkhas were unable to oppose the English, would lower the dignity of your name in the plains, and cause a reduction of your army to the extent of four thousand men. The enemy will moreover require the possession of Bisahur, and after that the conquest of Gurhwal will be easy; nor will it be possible, in that case, for us to retain Kumaon, and with it we must lose Dotee, Acham, and Joomlah, whence he may be expected to penetrate even to Bheree. If the English once establish themselves firmly in possession of a part of the hills, we shall be unable to drive them out: the countries towards the Sutlej should be obstinately defended; the abandonment of the disputed tracts in the plains is a lesser evil; the possession of the former preserves to us the road to further conquest.

You ought, therefore, to direct Gooroo Rungnath Pundit, and Dulbunjun Pandeh, to give up the disputed lands of Bootwul, Sheeoraj, and the twenty-two villages in the vicinity of Bareh, and thus, if possible, bring our differences to a termination. To this step I have no objections, and shall feel no animosity to those who may perform this service. I must, however, declare a decided hostility to such as, in bringing about a reconciliation with the English, consult only their own interest, and forget their duty to you. If they will not accept these terms, what have we to fear? The English attempted to take Bhurtpoor by storm; but the Raja Runjeet Singh destroyed a European regiment, and a battalion of sepoys. To the present day they have not ventured to meddle with Bhurtpoor again; whence it would seem that one fort has sufficed to check their progress.

In the low country of Dhurma they established their authority; but the Raja overthrew their army, and captured all their artillery and stores, and now lives and continues in quiet possession of his dominions. Our proffers of peace and reconciliation will be interpreted as the result of fear; and it would be absurd to expect that the enemy will respect a treaty concluded under such circumstances. Therefore, let us confide our fortunes to our swords; and, by boldly opposing the enemy, compel him to remain within his own territory—or, if he should continue to advance, stung with shame at the idea of retreating, after his immense preparations, we can then give up the lands in dispute, and adjust our differences.

Such, however, is the fame and terror of our swords, that Bulbhudur, with a force of six hundred men, defeated an army of three or four thousand English. His force consisted of the old Gourukh and Kurrukh companies, which were only partly composed of the inhabitants of our ancient kingdom, and of the people of the countries from Bheree to Gurhwal; and with these he destroyed one battalion, and crippled and repulsed another. My army is similarly composed; nevertheless, all descriptions are eager to meet the enemy. In your quarter you are surrounded with the veterans of our army, and cannot apprehend desertion from them: you have also an immense militia, and many Jageerdars, who will fight for their own honour and interests.

Assembling the militia of the low lands, and fighting in the plains, is impolitic—call them into the hills, and cut the enemy up by detail, (a passage here the sense of which cannot be discovered). The enemy is proud, and flushed with success, and has reduced under his subjection all the western Zemindars, the Ranas, and Raja of Kuhlor, and the Thakooraen, and will keep peace with no one. However, my advice is nothing. I will direct Ram Doss to propose to General Ochterlony the abandonment, on our part, of the disputed lands, and will forward to you the answer which he may receive. All the Ranas, Rajas, and Thakooraen, have joined the enemy, and I am surrounded; nevertheless, we shall fight and conquer, and all my officers have taken the same resolution. The Pundits have pronounced the month of *Bysakh*,* as particularly auspicious for the Goorkhas; and, by selecting a fortunate day, we shall surely conquer.

---

* Commencing about the 10th or 12th of April.

I am desirous of engaging the enemy slowly and with caution, but cannot manage it, the English being always first to begin the fight, I hope, however, to be able to delay the battle till *Bysakh*, when I will choose a favourable opportunity to fight them. When we shall have driven the enemy from hence, either Runjoor or myself, according to your wishes, will repair to your presence. In the present crisis, it is very advisable to write to the Emperor of China, and to the Lama of Lassa, and to the other Lamas; and for this purpose, I beg leave to submit the enclosed draft of a letter to their address; any errors in it, I trust, will be forgiven by you; and I earnestly recommend that you will lose no time in sending a petition to the Emperor of China, and a letter to the Lama.

Appendix 3

Treaty of Peace between the Honourable East India Com-
pany and Moha Raja Bickram Sah, Raja of Nepal, settled
between Lieutenant-Colonel Bradshaw, on the part of the
Honourable Company, in virtue of the full powers vested in
him by his Excellency the Right Honourable Francis, Earl of
Moira, Knight of the Most Noble Order of the Garter, one of
his Majesty's Most Honourable Privy Council, appointed by
the Court of Directors of the said Honourable Company to
direct and control all the affairs in the East Indies, and by Sree
Gooroo Gujraj Missur, and Chunder Seekur Opadheea, on
the part of Moharaja Kurman Jodh Bickram Sah Behaudur
Shumsheer Jung, in virtue of the powers to that effect vested in
them by the said Raja of Nepal.

Whereas war has arisen between the Honourable East
India Company and the Raja of Nepal, and whereas the
parties are mutually disposed to restore the relations of
peace and amity, which, previously to the occurrence of the
late differences, had long subsisted between the two states,
the following terms of peace have been agreed upon.

Article 1st—There shall be perpetual peace and friendship between the Honourable East India Company, and the
Raja of Nepal.

Article 2nd—The Raja of Nepal renounces all claim to
the lands which were the subject of discussion between the

two states before the war; and acknowledges the right of the Honourable Company to the sovereignty of those lands.

Article 3rd—The Raja of Nepal hereby cedes to the Honourable the East India Company, in perpetuity, all the under mentioned territories, namely:

First—The whole of the low lands between the rivers Kali and Raptee.

Secondly— The whole of the low lands (with the exception of Bootwul Khas) lying between the Raptee and the Gunduk.

Thirdly—The whole of the low lands between the Gunduk and Koosee, in which the authority of the British government has been introduced, or is in actual course of introduction.

Fourthly—All the low lands between the river Mechee and the Teesta.

Fifthly—All the territories within the hills, eastward of the river Mechee, including the fort and lands of Nagree, and the pass of Nagarcote, leading from Morung into the hills, together with the territory lying between that pass and Nagree.

The aforesaid territory shall be evacuated by the Goorkha troops within forty days from this date.

Article 4th—With a view to indemnify the chiefs and *barahdars* of the state of Nepal, whose interests will suffer by the alienation of the lands ceded by the foregoing article, the British government agrees to settle pensions, to the aggregate amount of two *lakh* of rupees per annum, on such chiefs as may be selected by the Raja of Nepal, and in the proportions which the Raja may fix. As soon as the selection is made, *Sunuds* shall be granted under the seal and signature of the Governor-General for the pensions respectively.

Article 5th—The Raja of Nepal renounces for himself, his heirs and successors, all claim to, or connexion with, the countries lying to the west of the river Kalee; and engages never to have any concern with these countries or the inhabitants thereof.

Article 6th—The Raja of Nepal engages never to molest or disturb the Raja of Sikhim in the possession of his territories; but agrees, if any differences shall arise between the state of Nepal and the Raja of Sikhim, or the subjects of either, that such differences shall be referred to the arbitration of the British government, by whose award the Raja of Nepal engages to abide.

Article 7th—The Raja of Nepal hereby engages never to take or retain in his service any British subject, nor the subject of any European or American state, without the consent of the British government.

Article 8th—In order to secure and improve the relations of amity and peace hereby established between the two states, it is agreed that accredited ministers from each shall reside at the court of the other.

Article 9th—This treaty, consisting of nine articles, shall be ratified by the Raja of Nepal within fifteen days from this date; and the ratification shall be delivered to Lieutenant-Colonel Bradshaw, who engages to obtain and deliver to the Raja the ratification of the Governor-General within twenty days, or sooner, if practicable.

Done at Segoulee, on the 2nd day of December, 1815

(L. S.) [Signed] *Paris Bradshaw*, Lt.-Col. P. A.

(L. S.) [Signed] *Gujraj Misur*

(L. S.) [Signed] *Chundur Seekhur Opadheea*

Received this treaty from Chundur Seekhur Opadheea,

agent on the part of the Raja of Nepal, in the valley of Muckwanpoor, at half-past two o'clock, p. m. on the 4th of March, 1816, and delivered to him the counterpart treaty on behalf of the British government.

[Signed] *D. Ochterlony*,
Agt. Governor-General.

Translation of an engagement (Ikrarnama) in the Hindee language, executed at Mukwanpoor Mandee, by Kajee Bukhtawur Singh Thapa, and Chundur Seekhur Opadheea, Plenipotentiaries on the part of the Raja of Nepal, and forwarded by General Sir David Ochterlony along with the above treaty.

At the time of delivering the treaty, Major-general Sir David Ochterlony was pleased to observe, that the Right Honourable the Governor-General had not authorised him to accept the treaty, and that he could not encourage any hope of those indulgences of which a prospect had been held out by Lieutenant-Colonel Bradshaw, being granted in addition to the treaty; that his Lordship indeed would not grant them, and that he (the General) would not recommend him to do so; that nothing beyond what was stated in the treaty would be allowed. Accordingly, we, Sree Kajee Bukhtawur Singh Thapa, and Chundur Seekhur Opadheea, have agreed to what Sir D. Ochterlony has required; in testimony whereof, we have executed this *Razeenama*, and delivered it to the Major-General, dated 5th of *Soodee Phagun*, 1872, *Sumbut*, corresponding with Tuesday the 4th of March, 1816.

A true Translation.
[Signed] *J. Monckton*
Persn. Secretary to Government.

From the Raja of Nepal, received on the 18th March, 1816

On the 21st of *Maug*, 1872, *Sumbut*, corresponding with the 2nd of February, 1816, I had the honour to receive your Lordship's letter, dated 13th of January, stating that it was your hope and expectation to have been able to address me in the language of friendship and congratulation, on the renewal of the former relations of amity between the British government and the state of Nepal; but that unfortunately that hope and that expectation had been defeated and frustrated by the extraordinary conduct adopted by my government, in refusing to ratify a solemn treaty concluded by my authorized agents, stated by myself and my ministers to have been vested with full powers; intimating, however, at the same time, that there was yet time to avoid the danger to which I had exposed myself, namely, that the instant ratification of the treaty, and its transmission to Major-General Sir David Ochterlony, would avert the impending evil, and would even induce your Lordship to consider the propriety of relaxing from the rigour of some parts of the engagement, but that any delay would be fatal; adding also, that your letter would be forwarded to me by the Major-General, who was vested with the command of the British force advancing into my territory, and with the conduct of all political affairs with my government.

The relations of harmony and friendship between the Honourable English Company and this state, by the favour of the British government, had subsisted without any difference of interest for a period of fifty years; and my ancestors were always grateful for its kindness. I also had no other wish but that of conforming to ancient rule; and the British government likewise conducted itself, as usual, in the spirit of kindness. Were I, indeed, to attribute the late transactions either to error on my side, or to unkindness on the part of the British government, I should be wrong—I ascribe all this war and tumult solely to the malignity of fortune. I nevertheless flattered myself that your Lordship still had my welfare at heart. Accordingly, when your Lordship addressed your letter of friendly admonition to me, I considered the counsel and advice which it contained to be all for my own good. I wished therefore, agreeably to your Lordship's injunctions, and for my own interests, to transmit the treaty by the hands of a confidential officer to Major-General Sir David Ochterlony; but, unfortunately, my evil destiny led me to delay its transmission; and, in the mean time, Sir David Ochterlony advanced with the British army to Mandee, near Muckwanpoor.

As I had no other object in view than the restoration of peace and friendship between the two states, I successively dispatched Kajee Bukhtawur Singh Thapa, and Chundur Seekhur Opadheea, with the ratified treaty to Sir David Ochterlony, who knowing your Lordship's favourable disposition towards me, and being himself also kindly disposed, opened a communication with Kajee Bukhtawur Singh, for the restoration of peace and amity, and received the treaty from the hands of that officer and Chundur Seekhur Opadheea; delivering to them at the same time, in exchange, for the purpose of being forwarded to me, the counterpart of it, under your Lordship's seal and signature, which I have since received.

Sir David Ochterlony caused Kajee Bukhtawur Singh, and Chundur Seekhur Opadheea, to execute a separate engagement in the Hindee language, (*Ikarnama*,) the contents of which will be made known to your Lordship by the Major-General's communications. I hereby confirm that engagement.

It only remains for me to express my hope that your Lordship will manifest your generosity and magnanimity in such a manner as to secure to this state the same rank and consideration which it has hitherto enjoyed: a compliance with this request is not inconsistent with the dictates of liberality and benevolence.

I trust that your Lordship, believing me to be ever anxious for the pleasing accounts of your health, will continue to gratify me by kind letters.

(A true Translation,)
[Signed] *J. Monckton*
Persn. Secretary to Government.

Appendix 4

Treaty, Covenant, or Agreement entered on by Captain Barre Latter, Agent on the part of his Excellency the Right Honourable the Earl of Moira, K. G. Governor-General, &c. &c. &c. and by Nazir Chama Tinjen, and Macha Timbah, and Lama Duchim Longdoo, deputies on the part of the Raja of Sickhimputee, being severally authorised and duly appointed for the above purposes.

Article 1st—The Honourable East India Company cedes, transfers, and makes over, in full sovereignty, to the Sikhimputee Raja, his heirs or successors, all the hilly or mountainous country situated to the eastward of the Mechee river, and to the westward of the Teesta river, formerly possessed and occupied by the Raja of Nepal, ceded to the Honourable East India Company by the treaty of peace signed at Segoulee.

Article 2nd—The Sikhimputee Raja engages, for himself and successors, to abstain from any acts of aggression or hostility against the Goorkhas, or any other state.

Article 3rd—That he will refer to the arbitration of the British government any disputes or questions that may arise between his subjects, and those of Nepal, or any other neighbouring state, and abide by the decision of the British government.

Article 4th—He engages for himself and successors to join the British troops with the whole of his military force,

153

when employed within the hills, and in general to afford the British troops every aid and facility in his power.

Article 5th—That he will not permit any British subject, nor the subject of any European or American state, to reside within his dominions without the permission of the English government.

Article 6th—That he will immediately seize and deliver up any *decoits*, or notorious offenders, that may take refuge within his territories.

Article 7th—That he will not afford protection to any defaulters of revenue, or other delinquents, when demanded by the British government through their accredited agents.

Article 8th—That he will afford protection to merchants and traders from the Company's provinces; and he engages that no duties shall be levied on the transit of merchandize beyond the established custom at the several *Golahs*, or marts.

Article 9th—The Honourable East India Company guarantees to the Sikhimputee Raja and his successors, the full and peaceable possession of the tract of hilly country specified in the first article of the present agreement.

Article 10th—This treaty shall be ratified and exchanged by the Sikhimputee Raja within one month from the present date, and the counterpart, when confirmed by his Excellency the Right Honourable the Governor-General, shall be transmitted to the Raja.

Done at Titalya, this 10th day of February, 1817, answering to the 9th of *Phagoon*, 1873, *Sumbut*, and to the 30th of *Maugh*, 1223, *Bengal* era.

LEONAUR

ALSO FROM LEONAUR
AVAILABLE IN SOFTCOVER OR HARDCOVER WITH DUST JACKET

SEPOYS, SIEGE & STORM *by Charles John Griffiths*—The Experiences of a young officer of H.M.'s 61st Regiment at Ferozepore, Delhi ridge and at the fall of Delhi during the Indian mutiny 1857.

CAMPAIGNING IN ZULULAND *by W. E. Montague*—Experiences on campaign during the Zulu war of 1879 with the 94th Regiment.

THE STORY OF THE GUIDES *by G. J. Younghusband*—The Exploits of the Soldiers of the famous Indian Army Regiment from the northwest frontier 1847 - 1900..

ZULU: 1879 *by D.C.F. Moodie & the Leonaur Editors*—The Anglo-Zulu War of 1879 from contemporary sources: First Hand Accounts, Interviews, Dispatches, Official Documents & Newspaper Reports.

THE RECOLLECTIONS OF SKINNER OF SKINNER'S HORSE *by James Skinner*—James Skinner and his 'Yellow Boys' Irregular cavalry in the wars of India between the British, Mahratta, Rajput, Mogul, Sikh & Pindarree Forces.

TOMMY ATKINS' WAR STORIES 14 FIRST HAND ACCOUNTS—Fourteen first hand accounts from the ranks of the British Army during Queen Victoria's Empire Original & True Battle Stories Recollections of the Indian Mutiny With the 49th in the Crimea With the Guards in Egypt The Charge of the Six Hundred With Wolseley in Ashanti Alma, Inkermann and Magdala With the Gunners at Tel-el-Kebir Russian Guns and Indian Rebels Rough Work in the Crimea In the Maori Rising Facing the Zulus From Sebastopol to Lucknow Sent to Save Gordon On the March to Chitral Tommy by Rudyard Kipling

CHASSEUR OF 1914 *by Marcel Dupont*—Experiences of the twilight of the French Light Cavalry by a young officer during the early battles of the great war in Europe.

TROOP HORSE & TRENCH *by R. A. Lloyd*—The experiences of a British Lifeguardsman of the household cavalry fighting on the western front during the First World War 1914-18.

THE EAST AFRICAN MOUNTED RIFLES *by C. J. Wilson*—Experiences of the campaign in the East African bush during the First World War.

THE FIGHTING CAMELIERS *by Frank Reid*—The exploits of the Imperial Camel Corps in the desert and Palestine campaigns of the First World War.

LEONAUR

ALSO FROM LEONAUR
AVAILABLE IN SOFTCOVER OR HARDCOVER WITH DUST JACKET

THE COMPLEAT RIFLEMAN HARRIS *by Benjamin Harris as told to & transcribed by Captain Henry Curling*—The adventures of a soldier of the 95th (Rifles) during the Peninsular Campaign of the Napoleonic Wars

WITH WELLINGTON'S LIGHT CAVALRY *by William Tomkinson*—The Experiences of an officer of the 16th Light Dragoons in the Peninsular and Waterloo campaigns of the Napoleonic Wars.

SERGEANT BOURGOGNE *by Adrien Bourgogne*—With Napoleon's Imperial Guard in the Russian Campaign and on the Retreat from Moscow 1812 - 13.

SWORDS OF HONOUR *by Henry Newbolt & Stanley L. Wood*—The Careers of Six Outstanding Officers from the Napoleonic Wars, the Wars for India and the American Civil War, with dozens of illustrations by Stabley L. Wood.

SURTEES OF THE RIFLES *by William Surtees*—A Soldier of the 95th (Rifles) in the Peninsular campaign of the Napoleonic Wars.

ENSIGN BELL IN THE PENINSULAR WAR *by George Bell*—The Experiences of a young British Soldier of the 34th Regiment 'The Cumberland Gentlemen' in the Napoleonic wars.

HUSSAR IN WINTER *by Alexander Gordon*—A British Cavalry Officer during the retreat to Corunna in the Peninsular campaign of the Napoleonic Wars.

NAPOLEONIC WAR STORIES *by Sir Arthur Quiller-Couch*—Tales of soldiers, spies, battles & sieges from the Peninsular & Waterloo campaingns.

JOURNALS OF ROBERT ROGERS OF THE RANGERS *by Robert Rogers*—The exploits of Rogers & the Rangers in his own words during 1755-1761 in the French & Indian War.

KERSHAW'S BRIGADE VOLUME 1 *by D. Augustus Dickert*—Manassas, Seven Pines, Sharpsburg (Antietam), Fredricksburg, Chancellorsville, Gettysburg, Chickamauga, Chattanooga, Fort Sanders & Bean Station..

KERSHAW'S BRIGADE VOLUME 2 *by D. Augustus Dickert*—At the wilderness, Cold Harbour, Petersburg, The Shenandoah Valley and Cedar Creek.

A TIGER ON HORSEBACK *by L. March Phillips*—The Experiences of a Trooper & Officer of Rimington's Guides - The Tigers - during the Anglo-Boer war 1899 - 1902.

LEONAUR

ALSO FROM LEONAUR

AVAILABLE IN SOFTCOVER OR HARDCOVER WITH DUST JACKET

THE COLLECTED SCIENCE FICTION AND FANTASY OF STANLEY G. WEINBAUM: INTERPLANETARY ODYSSEYS—Classic Tales of Interplanetary Adventure Including: A Martian Odyssey, its Sequel Valley of Dreams, the Complete 'Ham' Hammond Stories and Others.

THE COLLECTED SCIENCE FICTION AND FANTASY OF STANLEY G. WEINBAUM: OTHER EARTHS—Classic Futuristic Tales Including: Dawn of Flame & its Sequel The Black Flame, plus The Revolution of 1960 & Others.

THE COLLECTED SCIENCE FICTION AND FANTASY OF STANLEY G. WEINBAUM: STRANGE GENIUS—Classic Tales of the Human Mind at Work Including the Complete Novel The New Adam, the 'van Manderpootz' Stories and Others.

THE COLLECTED SCIENCE FICTION AND FANTASY OF STANLEY G. WEINBAUM: THE BLACK HEART—Classic Strange Tales Including: the Complete Novel The Dark Other, Plus Proteus Island and Others.

DARKNESS AND DAWN 1: THE VACANT WORLD by George Allen England—A Novel of a future New York.

DARKNESS AND DAWN 2: BEYOND THE GREAT OBLIVION by George Allen England—A Novel of a future America.

DARKNESS AND DAWN 3: THE AFTER GLOW by George Allen England—A Novel of a future America.

CARSON OF VENUS VOLUME 1: PIRATES OF VENUS & LOST ON VENUS—by Edgar Rice Burroughs—Two full length novels.

JOHN CARTER OF MARS VOLUME 1: THE PRINCESS OF MARS & THE GODS OF MARS—by Edgar Rice Burroughs—Two full length novels.

PELLUCIDAR - THE INNER WORLD VOLUME 1: AT THE EARTH'S CORE - PELLUCIDAR—by Edgar Rice Burroughs—Two full length novels.

BEFORE ADAM & OTHER STORIES—by Jack London—Includes the novel Before Adam + The Scarlet Plague A Relic of the Pliocene When the World Was Young and others.

THE IRON HEEL & OTHER STORIES—by Jack London—Includes the novel The Iron Heel + The Enemy of All the World The Shadow and the Flash The Strength of the Strong The Unparalleled Invasion The Dream of Debs.